MISEDUCATION

MISEDUCATION

Preschoolers at Risk

David Elkind

ALFRED A. KNOPF

New York 1987

THIS IS A BORZOI BOOK
PUBLISHED BY ALFRED A. KNOPF, INC.

Library of Congress Cataloging-in-Publication Data

Elkind, David.
Miseducation: preschoolers at risk.

Bibliography: p.
Includes index.
1. Education, preschool—United States.
2. Stress in children—United States. I. title.
LB1140.23.E43   1987   372'.21   86-82790
ISBN 0-394-55256-3   ISBN 0-394-75634-7 (pbk.)

Manufactured in the United States of America
First Edition

To my brothers, Jules, Ben, and Lee,
and to my sister, Kay,
with love and appreciation

Contents

Contents

HEALTHY EDUCATION

Acknowledgments

I HAVE BEEN working with nursery school children and their teachers and parents for more than a quarter of a century. Much of what I have learned during those years is distilled in this book, particularly the last five chapters. While it is not possible to acknowledge everyone individually, I do want to thank them collectively. In addition, I want especially to thank Marjorie Ford, the director of the children's school at Wheaton College, my first academic appointment, where I carried out my first studies on young children's thinking. With a great deal of patience, forgiving kindness, and expert knowledge, she taught me how to behave with young children, how to engage them in conversation, and how to appreciate their unique world-view. From Piaget I learned about how young children think, but from Marjorie Ford I learned about what young children feel and fantasy.

Writers live a great deal in their heads, which is often trying for those who care about them. I want to extend thanks and appreciation to my three sons, Paul, Robert, and Eric, not only for their patience with my mental as well as my physical lapses, but also for allowing me to use incidents from their childhood and for their support and encouragement of my work. But most of all, I owe a tremendous debt to my beloved wife, Nina, not only for her constant patience and generosity but also for her gracious forbearance in sharing her husband with a word-processor.

I would also like to thank Elizabeth Hall, my assistant at Tufts, for her many efforts, great and small, to keep my life organized and to protect my time. Last, but certainly not least, I want to thank Katherine Hourigan, the editor at Knopf who worked with me on the book through its several metamorphoses. Her gentle suggestions for revision, and patience with my resistance, helped give the book its final form and substance.

David Elkind
South Yarmouth, MA
Winter 1987

Preface

MORE THAN A DECADE ago I published a paper entitled "Early Childhood Education: Instruction or Enrichment." At that time I was concerned because some programs for young children were attempting to teach academic skills such as reading and math. By today's standards, the number of children affected was quite small, and the bulk of early-childhood programs had child-centered and age-appropriate curricula. After a few years I became involved in other issues, particularly the parental and social pressures on children and teenagers to grow up too fast too soon, and I published the results of my observations and research in two books, *The Hurried Child: Growing Up Too Fast Too Soon* and *All Grown Up and No Place to Go: Teenagers in Crisis*.

In the past few years, however, my attention has once again been drawn to what is happening in early-childhood education. Today it is not just the occasional preschool that is introducing academics to young children, it is the public school system as well. And it is not just academics that are being taught to young children but gymnastics, swimming, ballet, skiing, and karate. The minor ailment of a few preschools in the seventies has become an epidemic in the eighties.

At first, I thought that this was nothing more than a downward extension of the "hurrying" that I had written about in my earlier books. But as I listened to the parents whom I see in my small private practice and to the parents, educators, and health professionals I encounter when lecturing around the country, a somewhat different picture emerged. The parents who had had their first children in the early 1980s were quite different from the parents who had had their first children in the early 1970s. Whereas, in the past, parenting psychologies and practices might remain the same over decades, they now seem to be changing at a much faster rate, in a decade or less.

The parents who had their first children during the early seventies bear the psychic wounds of the extraordinary social revolution that changed our attitudes toward sex, marriage, divorce, and child-rearing. These challenges to fundamental values and beliefs required vast and far-reaching adjustments by the parents of that time, and all but exhausted parental energies for dealing with stress in general and the stress of child-rearing in particular.

In many ways, hurrying was a direct result of the fact that, after adapting to such enormous social changes, parents had few resources left to cope with the unending needs of children. Expecting, indeed demanding, that children grow up fast was one way of avoiding the expenditure of energy that goes along with parenthood. The media both reflected and encouraged this "hurrying" with its abundant images of "adultified" children. And the schools cooperated by downward extensions of the curriculum and test-driven instruction.

Hurrying children, expecting them to feel, think, and act much older than they are, stresses children. It puts extraordinary pressures upon them for adaptation. The consequences of hurrying are the usual symptoms of stress: headaches and stomachaches in preschoolers; learning problems and depression in elementary school children; and the whole gamut of teenage drug abuse, pregnancy, eating disorders, and suicide.

Whatever the problems stemming from his or her individual life history, the hurried young person is clearly responding as much to external pressures as to internal conflicts.

The dynamics of parents who miseducate their infants and young children, however, appear different from those that gave rise to hurrying. Many of the parents who engage in miseducation have grown up with the new values and do not experience the same conflicts and stresses of adjustment experienced by their parents. Young men and women today, for example, take current sexual mores and the new status of women as given because they have never known anything else. Although there are stresses, aplenty, parents who have their first children in the eighties generally do not undergo the conflicts of conscience experienced by parents of the seventies.

Whereas the parents who reared their children in the seventies felt overwhelmed and needed their children to grow up fast to reduce some of the pressure on themselves, parents today feel much more in charge of their lives and of their child-rearing. It is this sense of mastery, of being in charge and controlling things, which is so striking in the parents of this decade in contrast to those of the past decade. Parents today believe they can make a difference in their children's lives, that they can give them an edge that will make them brighter and abler than the competition. Parents who started out in the seventies hurry their children; parents of the eighties are miseducating theirs. Parents who started in the seventies need mature children, while parents of the eighties want superkids.

The effects of miseducation are also different from those of hurrying. For, while miseducation also stresses children, it does so in a different manner. A latchkey child, for example, is hurried because he or she is expected to cope with a difficult situation—being home alone for extended periods of time. Or a child who has to go to a baby-sitter and then a day-care center and then a baby-sitter again is hurried because the child has to make too many adaptations in too short a time. In many such cases, the parents have little if any choice in the matter, inasmuch as they may have to work and adequate child-care facilities are simply not available. Likewise, some single parents who use their child as a confidant usually do so out of a deep-seated need to share with somebody.

Compare these examples with an infant whose parent is attempting to teach him or her to read, to swim, or to do gymnastics. In this situation, the parent clearly has a choice and chooses to engage in practices that are more reflective of parental ego than of parental need. Although parents who miseducate their children may justify this on the basis that it is for the child's "own good," it is really parental "good" that is at issue. And this fact changes the effects of miseducation and makes them different from those of hurrying.

Infants and young children accept and participate in miseducation because it pleases those to whom they are attached, namely, their parents, not because they find it interesting or enjoyable. Miseducation can thus invoke internal conflicts and can set the groundwork for the more classical psychological problems such as neurosis and neurotic character formation. In some ways, miseducation is more pernicious than hurrying because it can lead to more deep-seated and less reversible problems than does hurrying. For example, some young people who have been hurried academically may take a year or two off after leaving college before getting on with their lives. But miseducation can leave the child with lifelong emotional disabilities.

I must say that I have had some trouble writing this book. As a father and as a family therapist who knows how difficult and unrewarding as well as rewarding parenting can be, I am generally sympathetic to parents. And I could empathize with parents who were hurrying their children because I knew their stresses first hand. But I have found it difficult to be sympathetic with parents who miseducate their children, because it is so unnecessary and so misguided.

Eventually I realized that today's parents are basically no different from parents of the past, and that there is a considerable overlap between hurrying and miseducating. Parenting styles are not new; they just recycle with changing times and are recycling faster today than ever before. In many ways, parents who miseducate their children are a reissue of the pre-hurrying parents who "spoiled" their children. Today's parents, like parents of the past, want to do what is best for their children and genuinely believe that early formal instruction is going to benefit their child. And today's parents, too, are victims of social pressure, of media oversell, and of the faddishness that marks educational practice in this country.

When I finally overcame my emotional block, I was at last able to sympathize with parents who miseducate their children and to write this book. My aim is to help parents of young children understand the dynamics of miseducation, the short- and long-term risks of such practices, and ways to identify healthy education in schools and to practice it at home. Although I am writing primarily for parents, I hope the book will also be helpful to teachers, administrators, and health professionals who work with young children and their families.

MISEDUCATION

1

Education and Miseducation

WHAT IS HAPPENING in the United States today is truly astonishing. In a society that prides itself on its preference for facts over hearsay, on its openness to research, and on its respect for "expert" opinion, parents, educators, administrators, and legislators are ignoring the facts, the research, and the expert opinion about how young children learn and how best to teach them.

All across the country, educational programs intended for school-aged children are being appropriated for the education of young children. In some states (for example, New York, Connecticut, and Illinois) educational administrators are advocating that children enter school at age four. Many kindergarten programs have become full-day kindergartens, and nursery school programs have become pre-kindergartens. Moreover, many of these kindergartens have introduced curricula, including work papers, once reserved for first-grade children. And in books addressed to parents a number of writers are encouraging parents to teach infants and young children reading, math, and science.

When we instruct children in academic subjects, or in swimming, gymnastics, or ballet, at too early an age, we miseducate them; we put them at risk for short-term stress and long-term personality damage for no useful purpose. There is no evidence that such early instruction has lasting benefits, and considerable evidence that it can do lasting harm.

Why, then, are we engaging in such unhealthy practices on so vast a scale? Like all social phenomena, the contemporary miseducation of large numbers of infants and young children derives from the coming together of multiple and complex social forces that both generate and justify these practices. One thing is sure: miseducation does not grow out of established knowledge about what is good pedagogy for infants and young children. Rather, the reasons must be sought in the changing values, size, structure, and style of American families, in the residue of the 1960s efforts to ensure equality of education for all groups, and in the new status, competitive, and computer pressures experienced by parents and educators in the eighties.

While miseducation has always been with us—we have always had pushy parents—today it has become a societal norm. If we do not wake up to the potential danger of these harmful practices, we may do serious damage to a large segment of the next generation.

THE EARLY-CHILDHOOD EDUCATION BOOM

Until the 1960s the education of young children was not regarded as a significant enterprise, and only a relatively small proportion of the early-childhood population attended nursery schools. The aim of early-childhood education was to provide enriched social and play experiences that children might not receive at home. It was assumed that such socialization and play fostered mental development as well, but this was seen as a by-product of the other nursery school activities. Nursery schools were regarded as providing social enrichment rather than intellectual stimulation.

Moreover, full-day out-of-home programs for young children (as provided by day-care centers) had acquired a stigma because they were known as places where children of family pathology (the children of unwed mothers or of incompetent or abusive parents) were looked after. And working women who had to put their children in one or another form of out-of-home program were either shunned as lacking in the maternal instinct or pitied because their husbands did not earn enough to support the family. It was widely believed that putting a young child in an out-of-home program on a regular basis for extended periods of time was harmful to the child.

As we shall see, however, the social revolutions of the 1960s effectively transformed our conception of out-of-home programs and of children's readiness to cope with and profit from such programs. The statistics tell the tale. In 1966 only 60 percent of five-year-olds attended kindergarten, while in 1985 82 percent of five-year-olds were attending public, private, or church-sponsored kindergarten programs.[1] Only twenty-five states provided aid for public kindergartens in 1965; by 1985 all fifty states were providing some form of public support for kindergarten and, increasingly, for pre-kindergarten programs as well.

The proliferation of educational programs for young children is not limited to five-year-olds. The number of nursery schools has increased a thousandfold since 1965, and the number of licensed day-care centers has grown 234 percent between 1978 and 1985. In 1985 some 2.5 million children (39 percent) attended pre-kindergarten programs compared to only 700,000 (11 percent) in 1965.[2] Never before in our history have so many of our infants and young children been enrolled for extended periods in regular out-of-home programs.

The Early-Childhood Debates

As the number of infants and young children enrolled in out-of-home programs has grown to include more than half of this population, the debates over whether or not such programs are beneficial or harmful have become more heated. On the one hand are psychologists such as Burton White and Raymond and Dorothy Moore, who argue that out-of-home programs are bad for young children and that at least one parent should stay home to rear and educate the child. White argues that this is necessary for the first three years; the Moores contend that children should be kept at home at least until the age of eight. At the other extreme are David Weikart and Alison Clarke-Stewart, who claim that out-of-home programs need not be harmful and can indeed be beneficial. White and the Moores tend to use research with middle-class children to support their arguments, while Weikart and Clarke-Stewart most often refer to work with children of low-income families.

Even among those who agree that out-of-home programs need not be harmful, there is still considerable debate over what kind of program is appropriate for young children. One group argues that young children in out-of-home settings should be exposed to formal education. In New York City, former Education Commissioner Gordon Ambach succeeded in making public kindergarten programs available for all four-year-old children whose parents need or want it. Twenty-four other states are currently considering kindergarten for four-year-olds.

Other writers, such as Yale psychologist Edward Zigler and a senior scientist for the Educational Testing Service, Irving Sigel, have argued for a preschool curriculum adapted to the learning abilities of young children, a curriculum that would not involve formal instruction in reading, math, and science. Again, the advocates of early instruction use research with disadvantaged youngsters to support their case whereas those opposed draw upon research with youngsters from all income levels.

There is also controversy among those who agree that young

children should be educated at home. On the one hand, writers such as Glenn Doman argue that parents should teach young infants to read and do math. On the other hand, writers such as Burton White argue that social interaction between parents and children is more significant for early learning than is the acquisition of specific skills, as advocated by Doman and others.

Not surprisingly, many parents experience these conflicting voices of experts more as a tower of Babel than as a source of guidance. That is the trouble with rapid social change. It can produce new social phenomena whose outcome is really problematic. What are parents to do? Whom should they listen to? What is best for their child and for them? While there is no simple answer to these questions, I believe that parents are best advised to go with the established authorities in the field rather than with those whose credentials are questionable and who stand to gain financially from the products or programs they endorse. And the professionals are solidly against miseducation:

> The philosophy of the American nursery school movement, which carries children up to kindergarten, never included the three R's. I firmly agree with this philosophy. In fact, it emphasizes that its only concern is with the physical, emotional, intellectual and social aspects of development which come before schooling. There are separate stages of development when each skill can be most readily acquired, and trying to hurry through them could easily misfire. In fact, experiments done years ago indicated that children who began reading at seven developed fewer reading problems than those who started at six.
>
> —BENJAMIN SPOCK,
> pediatrician and author of
> *Baby and Child Care*[3]

The whole range of normal child-care activities—cooing, rocking, feeding and playing—will naturally stimulate your baby.   —MICHAEL ROTHENBERG,
pediatrician and child psychiatrist,
University of Washington School of Medicine[4]

Most of the time, doing what comes naturally to you is exactly what your baby needs—whether it's cuddling, gazing into his or her eyes or trying to elicit a tiny grin.
—STANLEY GREENSPAN, M.D.,
chief of the Clinical Infant and Child Development
Research Center, National Institute
of Mental Health, and co-author of *First Feelings*[5]

The human infant is amazingly capable of compliance. He can be shaped to walk at nine months, recite numbers at two, read by three, and he can even learn to cope with the pressures that lie behind these expectations. But children in our culture need someone who will cry out, "At what price?"   —T. BERRY BRAZELTON,
pediatrician, author of *Toddlers and Parents*[6]

These high-powered schools with academic preschool programs are doing kids a disservice.   —IRVING SIGEL,
distinguished research scientist,
Educational Testing Service[7]

No authority in the field of child psychology, pediatrics, or child psychiatry advocates the formal instruction, in any domain, of infants and young children. In fact, the weight of solid professional opinion opposes it and advocates providing young children with a rich and stimulating environment that is, at the same time, warm, loving, and supportive of the child's own learning priorities and pacing. It is within this supportive, nonpressured environment that infants and young children acquire a solid sense of security, positive self-esteem, and a long-term enthusiasm for learning.

THE VARIETIES AND EXTENT OF MISEDUCATION

The threat of miseducation is greatest in public education, where the most children will be affected. And public education is increasingly guilty of putting children at risk for no purpose by exposing them to formal instruction before they are ready:

"Kindergarten classes are filling up once more. Parents are taking a hard look at the first year of school and demanding a greater stress on learning fundamentals. More are sending their children to preschool programs that launch four-year-olds armed with the alphabet. Schools are responding by fortifying the play-oriented kindergarten curriculum with weighty matters like arithmetic and reading. Parents now want their children to bring home a stack of papers," says Marilyn Arwood, principal of Waynewood Elementary School of Fairfax County, Virginia. "They want hard proof the child has learned something."[8]

Other developments in early public education include:

The age at which children start formal schooling is dropping. Now that kindergarten for 5-year-olds has become virtually universal in the nation's schools, demand is rising to make formal instruction available to all 4-year-olds.

Prekindergarten programs with heavy educational components for 3- and 4-year-olds are on the increase, especially for disadvantaged children.[9]

The boom in early-childhood education is, it very much appears, becoming a boom in miseducation. The extent of miseducation of young children has recently elicited a joint statement of concern by a group of national organizations involved in elementary and early-childhood education.[10] These organizations include the Association for Childhood Education International, Association for Supervision and Curriculum Development, International Reading Association, National Association for the Education of Young Children, National Association of Elementary School Principals, and National Council of Teachers of English.

Some of the concerns mentioned in the joint statement were as follows:

1. Many pre-first-grade children are subjected to rigid formal prereading programs with inappropriate expectations and experiences for their level of development.

2. Little attention is given to individual development and individual learning styles.

3. The pressures of accelerated programs do not allow children to be risk takers as they experiment with language and internalize concepts about how language operates.

4. Too much attention is focused upon isolated skill development or abstract parts of the reading process, rather than upon the integration of oral language, writing, and listening with reading.

5. Too little attention is placed upon reading for pleasure; therefore children do not associate reading with enjoyment.

Each of these concerns is centered on one or another facet of miseducation, the many ways we can place children at risk for learning problems to no purpose. The potential dangers of the miseducation practices described above far outweigh any potential gains.

It is not only the schools that are introducing formal instruction to young children; parents are doing so as well. Parents have been barraged with commercial programs and books which promise them that if they follow certain procedures they can not only teach infants and young children reading and math, but also make their offspring brighter and raise their IQ—in a phrase, make them "superkids."

The best-known and best-publicized of these "superkid" practices are those of Glenn Doman, whose books *Teach Your Baby to Read*, *Teach Your Baby Math*, *How to Multiply Your Baby's Intelligence*, and *How to Give Your Baby an Encyclopedic Mind* have sold hundreds of thousands of copies. More than three thousand parents from all over the country, and the world, have spent a week (at a cost of $490) at Doman's Better Baby Institute to learn the teaching techniques he claims will make any child into a prodigy. In addition to the course, parents can also purchase videotapes and teaching materials.

In his book on teaching babies how to read, Doman describes the first step in teaching an infant to read and become a "superkid":

> Now simply hold up the word mummy, just beyond his reach, and say to him clearly, "This says Mummy."
>
> Give the child no more description and do not elaborate. Permit him to see it for ten seconds.
>
> Now play with him, give him your undivided affection for a minute or two, then present the word again for the second time. Again, allow him to see it for ten seconds, again tell him just once in a clear voice, "This says Mummy."
>
> Now play with him again for two minutes.
>
> Again show him the card for ten seconds, again repeat that it is "Mummy."
>
> Do not ask him what it is.
>
> The first lesson is now over and you have spent less than five minutes.[11]

Doman is hardly alone in his promise that his form of early instruction can make children brighter. In their book *Give Your Child a Superior Mind*, Siegfried and Therese Engelmann argue that preschool children can learn to read, add, subtract, multiply, count, spell, and tell time. Unlike Doman, who claims that young children learn faster than older children and adults, the Engelmanns argue that young children learn more slowly than they will at a later age.

Their teaching procedure is also different from Doman's. Whereas Doman is very time-oriented, the Engelmanns are more concerned with the sequence in which materials are presented. Here is an example of the procedures they claim will teach a child to read and to increase his or her IQ:

> When you presented objects during the child's first eighteen months of life, you generally followed this procedure:
>> Isolate the object
>> Name the object
>> Require the child to point to the object
> As he becomes more verbal you should expand this procedure:
>> Isolate the object
>> Name the object
>> Require the child to repeat the name
>> Require the child to name the object as you point.[12]

In *Raising Brighter Children*, Sidney Ledson offers still another approach to producing superkids. Unlike Doman and the Engelmanns, who seem to use the whole-word method for teaching reading and brightness, Ledson suggests that parents teach young children phonics:

> Traditionally, the first letter children have been taught is the letter A. There is, however, no inherent fitness to A. Our purpose is better served here if the letter C is the first one taught. Show your child the letter C on page 69 and tell him the shape tells him to make the throat clearing sound (but not necessarily using the words shape or sound in your instruction) a sort of Kuh sound, but without grunt

or voice being given to the uh part. Just say, "This tells us to say Kuh, Edwina." Encourage the child to make the sound while tracing her finger around the shape of the letter a few times.[13]

A last example: in *How to Have a Smarter Baby*, Dr. Susan Ludington-Hoe advises parents of six-month-old infants to engage them in "Abstract Games That Build Abstract Thinking Ability."

> Abstract thinking games are ideal this month. Start by naming familiar objects in your home. Baby's blanket. His black and white bear. His high chair. When you meet them during your daily routine you can address them with a friendly "Hello, Blankie." Eventually as you name objects, baby will reach for them when they are in sight. Later you will find that he can be sitting in the middle of the floor, paying attention to another toy, when you say "Dog!" He'll look around for the dog you've mentioned. Then you'll know that he has attained a true understanding of object permanence and has learned that words represent objects.[14]

Nothing new is offered in these books or in others like them. The authors are merely extending well-known learning principles downward to infants and young children or formalizing procedures parents use spontaneously when they interact with their offspring. There is absolutely no evidence that such teaching gives children any lasting advantage in reading or that it has any effect on a child's brightness. There is evidence, however, as we shall see, that too early formal instruction can do harm.

The miseducation of infants and young children is not limited to unwarranted efforts to teach them academics; it has extended to all facets of young children's development. The idea that young children can benefit from a program of formal instruction has spread to sports and to exercise, to music and gymnastics, to ballet, beauty contests, and karate. Done well, with a sensitivity to children's physical and intellectual limitations and to their psychological vulnerability, such programs need not necessarily be harmful. Nonetheless, because such programs put infants and young children in inappropriate learning situations, they also put them at risk of physical and/ or psychological damage—and this despite the fact that such programs have no proven long-term benefit for youngsters.

The proliferation of commercial, formal instructional exercise programs for infants and young children is witness to our new eagerness to extend formal instruction to this age group. Across the country, infants as young as two or three months are being enrolled in fitness classes. Baby gyms with names like Gymboree, Playorama, Exercise Plus, and Great Shapes have prospered. Parents are told that such programs have both physical and psychological benefits. According to Suzy Prudden, author of *Suzy Prudden's Exercise Program for Young Children*:

> Exercise at an early age gently stretches the pectoral muscles, allowing the chest to expand, and creates much more room for the lungs to inhale and exhale. Circulation is increased, sending oxygen to the brain. Muscle strength is improved.[15]

While this statement is true, it is also true that most infants can get all the exercise and the benefits described above simply by crawling on the floor, reaching for objects, pulling themselves up on the side of the crib, and so on. As social activities, for parents and their infants, such exercise classes may have some value, but if the exercises are too strenuous (always a possibility when adults are setting goals for little ones), there is real danger of physical harm. And if parents become too intense about success and failure, psychological harm is possible as well.

Swimming classes for infants and young children have become widespread, sometimes sponsored by the YM/YWCA. Again, as social activities in which parent and child can participate together, the classes may have some value. But there are risks involved as well. Infants in swimming classes are at risk for middle-ear infections and potential permanent hearing loss, for autoasphyxiation from swallowing water, and for diarrhea, since the babies are not toilet-trained and the water may be polluted. Nonetheless, some of those who promote such training target their appeal to parental anxieties. In her book *Watersafe Your Baby in One Week*, Danuta Rylko says:

> Every day, the newspaper tells stories of small children losing their lives in their own backyard swimming pools. And every time I read one of these stories, my heart aches for that child and those parents, because the tragedy and the agony could have been avoided. There is no reason for a conscious child to drown. Teaching a child to save his life in any body of water is a relatively simple procedure. . . . You can teach an infant as young as 4 months to hold his breath, to surface after a tumble into a pool, to turn on his back and breathe and relax and float . . . indefinitely . . . for hours if necessary—until help arrives.[16]

Perhaps in areas where many people have swimming pools such an appeal has some virtue. But the mother of a nine-month-old child who lives in Boston (where backyard swimming pools are uncommon) told me that many of her friends were putting their babies into swimming classes and were urging her to do likewise. She declined because she was aware of some of the risks that I mentioned earlier. One of her friends got so worked up at her refusal that she demanded, "Do you want your baby to drown?" What is most disturbing about such a remark is the idea that parental responsibility lies in teaching an infant to swim rather than in making sure the baby is never in danger of drowning. But it is not the baby's responsibility not to drown! It is our job as responsible adults not to let a baby drown.

ARGUMENTS FOR THE FORMAL INSTRUCTION OF YOUNG CHILDREN

In Chapter 3 we will look at some of the professional arguments for the formal instruction of young children in the schools and how these derived from the social activist mood of the 1960s rather than from the actual science of that time or of the present. But there have always been popular arguments for the efficacy of early instruction in the home which often seem quite convincing but which do not hold up under close examination.

One popular argument cites examples of men and women of eminence who received early instruction: John Stuart Mill, the philosopher; the cyberneticist Norbert Wiener; Jeremy Bentham, jurist and philosopher; Thomas Babington Macaulay, English historian, poet, and statesman; Gottfried Wilhelm von Leibnitz, German philosopher and mathematician. But there are several problems with these examples. In the first place, one can find many people of eminence who did not have early instruction by parents: Einstein, Darwin, Marx, Freud, Piaget, Edison, Georgia O'Keeffe, and Eleanor Roosevelt are just a few. If early instruction is so crucial to the attainment of eminence, how did these men and women attain greatness?

Second, many children who are gifted intellectually or with talent *demand* stimulation from their parents at an early age; they gobble up information and are insatiable in their quest for knowledge about the world or for opportunities to exercise their talent in art, music, or writing. If early instruction had an impact upon youngsters such as John Stuart Mill and Norbert Wiener, it may well have been because they were gifted to begin with; had they been less receptive, their parents might well have given up. Indeed, the proponents of early instruction fail to mention the many parents who have attempted to produce brighter children through early instruction and have failed.

Finally, the parents of famous children who instructed them at an early age all did so in different ways, with different methods, and in different degrees. Blaise Pascal was taught by his father, but Goethe attended a nursery school. John Stuart Mill's father taught him Greek and Latin, while Leibnitz's father attempted to instill a love of history in his young son. Mozart toured Europe as a *Wunderkind*, which provided yet another type of stimulation and instruction. If early instruction succeeds in producing superkids, what type is it to be, when should it be begun, and who should do it? As we have seen, even the contemporary advocates of early instruction such as Doman and the Engelmanns differ greatly in the methods they propose.

The major difficulty with these accounts of the early instruction of eminent people is that they are largely anecdotal. A recent systematic study of gifted and talented people by Benjamin Bloom and his colleagues does not support the view that eminence in any particular field is largely a matter of whether or not the child received early instruction. These investigators examined 120 talented and successful people to ascertain what in their backgrounds could be held responsible for their outstanding attainments.

Consider the twenty research mathematicians whose careers they explored. All the mathematicians were under forty, had won Sloan Foundation Fellowships, and were generally recognized by their colleagues as outstanding. The parents of

these mathematicians were themselves of above-average intellectual ability, as evidenced by the level of their educational
attainments:

> The parents of the twenty mathematicians included in this
> study were well educated. Fourteen (70%) of the fathers
> had advanced degrees: Five earned Ph.D.s, three M.D.s
> and two law degrees. Three of the remaining six attended
> college, whereas the other three did not go beyond high
> school. Eleven (55%) of the mothers earned at least one
> college degree, four more had some college experience and
> all but one of the remaining five had graduated from high
> school. Reaching such levels of educational attainment was
> especially noteworthy because those parents who went to
> college generally did so during the Depression, often going
> to night school or extending their education over several
> years because of the necessity to work. Even so, several
> managed to distinguish themselves. One father was a Rhodes
> Scholar and several of the parents graduated with honors.[17]

These parents were bright, and the chances of having a
bright or exceptionally bright offspring were much better than
average. Even more important, from the perspective of the
present discussion, was the attitude of these parents toward
early intervention:

> The parents of the mathematicians believed it would be
> wrong to direct the interests of their children. They report
> trying to treat them as "normal."
> "I think it is a waste to try and make a child into
> something you want rather than providing them with the
> things they are interested in and letting them become what
> they want to." (Mother of M4)
> "I have strong feelings against pressuring children and
> tailoring them to fit parental expectations." (Mother of M21)

"We tried to protect him and to make him normal . . . the idea was to see if I could have a bright child who was well adjusted, getting along with people, having friends, having a lot of interests—not being single minded." (Mother of M17)[18]

None of the parents of the 120 subjects were pushy. During the early years, much of their teaching and learning was playful:

> The available piano was a toy for all but one of the pianists. Some children were propped up as infants and encouraged or allowed to play at the keyboard. Others began by toddling to the piano and "plunkin' on the keys as much with the palms of my hands as with my fingers, then running to Mother and saying, 'Was that a nice song?' and then going back and doing it some more." Another "played around on the keyboard making sound effects of thunder and lightning."[19]

This study of gifted and talented people who were successful adults gives no support to the idea that early formal instruction creates intellectual giftedness or creative talent. Rather, what is consistent in these autobiographical statements is that the parents of people who have attained eminence were careful not to impose their own priorities on their children but, instead, to follow each child's lead. In this regard, and in their concern with having their children be well-rounded persons, these parents are exponents of healthy, child-centered early-childhood education.

A recent study of the MacArthur Fellows[20] reinforces the findings from the Bloom investigation.

The John D. and Catherine T. MacArthur Foundation of Chicago has identified over one hundred persons whose creative lives have shown the fertility we normally associate with the able learner, especially the gifted and talented. The range of their abilities is enormous. They are artists—writers, musicians, filmmakers. They observe human behavior—as anthropologists, historians, psychologists. They follow abstract scientific theory—in chemistry, biology, mathematics, astrophysics. Their fields vary from the familiar—education, philosophy, the law—to the offbeat—Mayan hieroglyphics, book design.

The MacArthur Fellows are hand-picked. About one hundred anonymous nominators or "talent scouts" search for individuals of extraordinary promise. A committee of fifteen meets monthly to review the nominations, and the foundation calls the selected artists and scholars to inform them they have been chosen to receive awards ranging from $24,000 to $60,000 annually for a period of five years. The MacArthur Fellows submit no applications. They draw up no special plans or projects. They are not expected to submit reports or to publish results. They have qualified for the awards by uncommon abilities, demonstrated across a wide spectrum of creative pursuits.

The investigators sent all of the MacArthur Fellows a nine-item questionnaire, to which about half (fifty) responded. One of the questions was whether or not their parents were unusually supportive, and the investigators concluded: "If there is a single theme which threads through the responses and strings them together it is the crucial role of home life and parental guidance in shaping these unusually creative minds."[21]

Several typical answers:

Sylvia Law: "Although my parents were not well educated, I believe the dinner table conversation was far more significant in instilling both social values and concern for knowledge and facts."[22]

Francesca Rochberg Halton: "I was very close to my parents and they were unusually supportive. I read a lot at home because I saw them reading all of the time, and I suppose that helped at school."[23]

The investigators also concluded that "although supportive, the parents of the MacArthur Fellows appear not to have applied unreasonable pressure."[24]

Again, some typical responses:

Stephen Barry said that his parents never pushed him, "but they were quite ready, perhaps exceptionally ready, to allow me to pursue my own interests."[25]

William Clark: "I grew up in a house full of books and journals and newspapers and a continuing discussion of the things in them as though they mattered. All of this was very low key, and as far as I can tell the only pressures on me were self-imposed."[26]

Robert Root Bernstein: "The most important educational influences in my life were undoubtedly my parents. Their philosophy was to make available whatever 'learning tools' one desired ('learning tool' to be interpreted as broadly as possible) when one desired them. For example, both my brother and I learned to play musical instruments, but only after we asked to do so."[27]

From these findings, and from the findings of the study of individuals who attained eminence early, we can draw several conclusions. Certainly parents play a crucial role in the lives of individuals who are intellectually gifted or creatively talented. But this role is not one of active instruction, of teaching children skills, such as advocated by Doman, the Engelmanns, and Ledson. Rather, it is the support and encouragement parents give children and the intellectual climate that they create in the home which seem to be the critical factors.

Another finding is of relevance here, one often reported in the autobiographies of people who have attained eminence despite poor beginnings. The first mentor of these outstanding people was not someone who taught them the skills of their discipline or craft but always someone with tremendous enthusiasm for his field, even though not necessarily proficient in it. What these gifted and talented people took from this first mentor was a tremendous excitement, commitment, and involvement with what was to be their life's work. Mentors who taught them the skills of their craft only came later in their careers.

These findings point up the fallacy of early instruction as a way of producing children who will attain eminence. Miseducation, in fact, reverses the natural order of development. With gifted and talented individuals, as with children in general, the most important thing is an excitement about and enthusiasm for learning. Skills are easily learned when the motivation is there. Miseducation, by focusing upon skills to the detriment of motivation, pays an enormous price for teaching infants and young children what amounts to a few tricks. An ounce of motivation is worth a pound of skills anytime.

Another popular argument for early instruction is that children now are intellectually more able at earlier ages because of the modern technology with which they are surrounded. With television, even young children have immediate access to all sorts of information, about foreign places and peoples, about space exploration and deep-sea expeditions. Likewise, the presence of computers in homes and preschools means that children are growing up with this modern marvel and will necessarily be more sophisticated in its use than would earlier generations. If parents don't create superkids, then modern technology does.

Actually, this argument has two parts, one having to do with the direct impact of technology itself and the other with the indirect effect of the information conveyed by that technology.

In response to the first half of the argument, there is no evidence that early exposure to a technology in any way accelerates mental development. The overall direct effect of technology on human nature is to extend and amplify but not alter our biological capacities. Machines extend and amplify the strength of our muscles, telephones extend and amplify our hearing, telescopes and microscopes extend and amplify our vision, while computers extend and amplify our memory.

What has to be emphasized is that such extensions and amplifications do not change our biological potential. Eyeglasses do not improve our visual system any more than a hearing aid enhances our auditory system. In the same way, a computer does not increase our ability to remember any more than using a lever makes us stronger. And, fortunately, the power of modern weaponry has not increased our aggressiveness.

Now for the second part of the argument. If technology does not directly improve our sensory or motor capacities, doesn't it do so indirectly through the information it provides? Doesn't this information improve our brains and make us more sophisticated and knowledgeable than if we did not have the technology?

To be sure, there is a point here. Children today do indeed have access to more information than did children of earlier generations. Yet many years ago John Dewey wrote that learning is the "representation of experience," by which he meant that experience, raw information, does not teach in and of itself. It is only when we talk about and reflect upon the experience or information we receive that we learn from it. While it is certainly true that children today are exposed to much more information than ever before, that exposure in and of itself does not guarantee that children will learn from the information if it is not talked about and examined.

For children really to profit from the barrage of information to which they are exposed, they must also be given the time and opportunity to reflect upon that experience. Yet parents today are spending less time talking with their children than in the past. A recent survey[28] conducted by the Institute for Social Research at the University of Michigan makes the point. The investigators defined quality-time activities as reading to the children, conversing with them, or playing with them.

The findings were striking. Working mothers spend only an average of eleven minutes each weekday doing such things and thirty minutes per day on weekends. Homemaker mothers did spend more time this way, devoting thirty minutes each weekday and thirty-six minutes each weekend day to their offspring. Fathers, mostly employed outside the home, spend even less quality time with their children than working mothers do; they devoted a scant eight minutes to their kids each weekday and only fourteen minutes on weekends. And the way the fathers spend their time is not affected by whether their wives work or not.

If children do not have the opportunity to talk about and reflect upon their experiences, they are not likely to learn from them. So while it is true that children are exposed to more information and a greater variety of experiences than were children of the past, it does not follow that they automatically become more sophisticated. We always know much more than we understand, and with the torrent of information to which young people are exposed, the gap between knowing and understanding, between experience and learning, has become even greater than it was in the past.

In short, neither of the popular arguments advanced by those who advocate early instruction as the means to producing brighter, more gifted children can really stand close analysis. The anecdotal case histories of men such as John Stuart Mill are not supported by systematic research on the gifted and talented, which clearly shows that they were not pushed in the early years. Likewise, the fact that children today grow up with more advanced technology than young people in previous generations does not accelerate their mental growth. Nor do they become genuinely more sophisticated because of the avalanche of information to which they are exposed. As far as intellectual development and sophistication go, children today are basically no different from children of fifty or one hundred years ago.

THE WORLD OF THE YOUNG CHILD

It is all too easy for us as adults to forget just how inexperienced infants and young children really are and how much they have to learn about the world that we have already conceptualized and now take for granted. Once we recognize how much time and energy infants and young children must expend in constructing a world of objects, sights, sounds, colors, shapes, relationships of up and down, of behind and on top of, plants, animals, trees, and much, much more, the fallacy of miseducation becomes obvious.

Infants and young children are not just sitting twiddling their thumbs, waiting for their parents to teach them to read and do math. They are expending a vast amount of time and effort in exploring and understanding their immediate world. Healthy education supports and encourages this spontaneous learning. Early instruction miseducates, not because it attempts to teach, but because it attempts to teach the wrong things at the wrong time. When we ignore what the child has to learn and instead impose what we want to teach, we put infants and young children at risk for no purpose.

THE SOCIAL DYNAMICS OF MISEDUCATION

2

Superkids:
Miseducation Parent Style

PARENTS TODAY ARE more concerned that their children be "special" than that they be "average" or "normal." In the past, parents were usually relieved to learn that their children were doing what they should be doing at a particular age. No more! Today's parents want their youngsters to excel, to be the best. And there is certainly nothing wrong with wanting our children to do well; a parent who did not want successful children would certainly be suspect. In the past, however, this interest in having special children was balanced by an equally powerful concern about the children's emotional health and a fear that pushing exceptionality at a tender age would lead to neurosis. "Early Ripe, Early Rot," as the saying went.

Today's parents are equally concerned about their children's mental health, but in contrast to the parents of the baby boomers, contemporary parents believe that exceptional early achievement will enhance their children's self-esteem and self-confidence and give them a "leg up" on the competition. A constant theme of those advocating early academics, early sports, and early artistic instruction is that it not only promotes exceptionality, but has important positive benefits for children's personality development as well.

The contemporary concern with exceptionality (with having superkids) stems from a variety of factors and causes. First of all, our families today are smaller, and parents feel considerable pressure to do a good job with their child or children because they have so little margin for error. Then too, having a child in today's world is very expensive (in 1986, the total cost of rearing a child was estimated at upwards of $143,000), and parents want to have something special to show for that investment. And the current "brain" race both within and between countries also helps drive parents to make their child as bright as possible.

Other factors include the notion of the "competent child" that professionals popularized in the 1960s. Unfortunately, parents are about ten years behind the professionals: many of the advocates of early instruction, such as Benjamin Bloom and Jerome Bruner, have considerably modified their positions. But this change in the thrust of professional opinion has received nowhere near the degree of media attention that has been accorded to "child competence." Many of my college students, for example, have trouble understanding why it is not possible to teach academics to infants and young children, just because they have been brought up on the conception of the competent child.

Yet another dynamic is the social pressure which leads parents to be more competitive with respect to their children than ever before. The unfortunate end result of this competitive urge is reinforcement of the belief that "earlier is better." Starting earlier, today's parents believe, is the best way to give their child an edge against the competition.

It is this combination of factors, then, which has given rise to the parental pressure, sometimes conscious, sometimes unconscious, for superkids. But children cannot be exceptional in all domains, and parents have to be selective. The particular area in which they push their child for exceptionality reflects a complex of parental personality dynamics that comes together in a special family and parenting style. While I will describe these styles as separate and distinct, in truth there is a little of each style in each of us. And no one style is necessarily better or worse than another. What does harm is the imposition of these family styles on children at too early an age, which constitutes miseducation. It is the "superkid" psychology that accounts for much of the miseducation practiced by parents today.

GOURMET PARENTS

Some young couples have achieved occupational and financial success. They are able to afford a nice home, expensive cars, and frequent vacations to exotic places: they have attained what in Western society is now regarded as an enviable lifestyle. Such parents pursue their careers with great energy and admirable self-discipline: working long hours, but also exercising regularly and watching their diet. Both at work and away from work, they are careful to obey the principles of decorum in dress, language, and behavior. They achieved their success, as the saying goes, the hard way: they worked for it.

When Gourmet couples become parents, they often adopt toward child-rearing the same methods they did toward their careers: just as they groomed themselves for a successful career, so they groom themselves to become successful parents. They read the latest books on child-rearing and attend lectures and classes on child development. Gourmet parents believe they can do as good a job in child-rearing as they did in shaping their careers, and a superkid is proof of their parenting prowess.

Gourmet parents dress young children in the most expensive designer clothes, enroll them in the most prestigious classes and programs, and buy them elaborate electronic toys and equipment. Three-year-olds accompany their parents on trips to Europe and to expensive restaurants. By five years of age many children of such parents have traveled more than many adults. The child of Gourmet parents far surpasses the norm of sophistication for his or her age group.

> As their elders relive the childhood joys of biking, some young children are climbing behind the wheel of their own automobiles. Precocious tots, especially in California, are tooling around driveways and parks in faithfully down-sized versions of Porsches, Ferraris and other exotic cars driven by their parents. . . . One line of kiddie luxury cars, produced in Italy by Agostini Autojunior, features leather seats, hydraulic disc brakes and two-speed stick shifts. Powered by a 3-h.p. lawnmower type engine, the little cars provide a foretaste of life in the fast track.[1]

Here is a classic case of Gourmet parents from my files. Hal and Margaret J. established a successful law firm in Boston. Both had come from lower-middle-class working families, attended public schools and the state university, and helped support themselves through college by working part-time. They met at law school and married shortly after they graduated. After their practice was established, they decided to have children. They wanted two, a boy and a girl. They arranged that Margaret would give birth during the summer months when business was slow and when she could afford to take a couple of months off.

Everything worked pretty much as planned. The first baby, a seven-pound boy, arrived in July, and Margaret was back at work by the end of September. They were fortunate in finding a retired woman who was willing to live in during the week to take care of Joshua. From the start, Margaret was alert to all of the latest theories on child psychology and child-rearing. At six months of age, Joshua was on the waiting list for a prestigious nursery school. Margaret insisted on having

Josh in swimming classes and was looking forward to putting him into a foreign language course when he was two. He had the most modern and advanced toys, including a toy computer. At two, Joshua accompanied his parents to Aspen, and at three he was fitted out with his own ski clothes and began taking skiing lessons.

When I saw Josh, he was five years old and was being expelled from his kindergarten class. He had not been accepted at the prestigious nursery school because he was not toilet-trained by three and a half. At school he was self-centered and overbearing, unwilling to share or to play cooperatively. If he was frustrated, he threw a tantrum and fell screaming to the floor. His parents had absolutely no control over him and were victims of his whims. They did not know where they had gone wrong. It never occurred to them that child-rearing is not the same as pursuing a career or that they were giving their child very mixed messages about what they expected of him.

In many ways, of course, Josh resembles an old-fashioned case of "spoiling." But Josh was not merely indulged; he was also pressured to achieve in a number of different areas, such as skiing and swimming. What happened, of course, was that the parents left the discipline and the limit-setting to the baby-sitter and to the instructors while they themselves indulged and pampered him. Because the parents did not set limits and controls, Josh could not accept them from other adults.

In many cases, Gourmet parents come from humble beginnings that often provided the motivation to work hard and achieve more. Gourmet parents seem to want it both ways: wanting their children to enjoy the fruits of their success, but also to acquire the motivation to achieve success on their own. By exposing children to the values and trappings of an affluent life-style too early, however, they may do the opposite: they may undermine their children's budding sense of autonomy and self-esteem, and the children may come to think of themselves in terms of what they have and whom they can control rather than who they are as individuals.

COLLEGE-DEGREE PARENTS

Another group of middle-class parents, often involved in education or related fields such as publishing, believe that a solid liberal arts education, crowned by a bachelor's degree, is the foundation for a full and successful life. But College-Degree parents may also be caught up in the "superkid" syndrome and want to rear a child who is exceptionally bright and exceptionally advanced academically. The way to achieve this exceptionality, they feel, is to start the child as early as possible in academics—reading, math, the classics, and science. College-Degree parents want their child to attend a prestigious preschool, in part at least because acceptance in such a preschool is proof of the child's above-the-norm status.

College-Degree parents are very much concerned with the curriculum taught in preschools and the early school grades. One College-Degree parent, for example, asked the prospective nursery school director, "What is your science curriculum?" Another screamed at her child's first-grade teacher, "You can't give him a 'satisfactory.' How will he ever get into MIT?" Many College-Degree parents want their children to bring workpapers home from the nursery school. They become more than a little troubled when they visit a nursery school where children are busy at dramatic play, sitting in chairs in a row while the "conductor," seated in the first chair with a cake pan for a steering wheel, takes his bus through town! Such activities clearly do not offer a sufficient academic challenge to their intellectually gifted offspring.

Many College-Degree parents have had parents who emphasized the value of education: it was the path of upward mobility, the way to get ahead and to fulfill the American dream. In many ways it still is, but there is a fundamental difference between the way College-Degree parents were brought up and the way they are bringing up their own children. It is not the value of education that is in question here but, rather, the respective responsibilities of the parents and the children for that education.

In an earlier era, parents who valued education saw their own role as an enabling one, making it possible for their children to have an education they themselves did not have. That orientation still exists among children of certain immigrants and among working-class parents. But the "superkid" psychology has introduced a subtle but all-important change in parental orientation. College-Degree parents see the parental role no longer as "making it possible" for children to have an education but more as giving them an "edge."

Part of the "superkid" psychology is that parents play an important part in getting their children to excel. By getting their young child into an academically oriented preschool and/ or by teaching the child to read early, College-Degree parents hope to give their child superior intellectual ability. What is wrong with that, any reasonable person might ask? What is wrong is that it involves a subtle shift of responsibility from the child to the parent. If our children succeed academically, it is because of our teaching and because we got them into the right schools at the right time. Yet if children fail to do well, it is of course the children's fault, because they were given everything needed to attain intellectual superiority and didn't exploit it. The problem with parents giving children the ingredients for intellectual superiority is that they can take credit for the children's success while denying any responsibility for their failure.

A couple of extreme examples of parents taking responsibility for their children's accomplishments highlight the risks of trying to create superkids. One is a reminiscence of John Stuart Mill:

> I remember the very place in Hyde Park where, in my fourteenth year, on the eve of leaving my father's house for a long absence, he told me that I should find, as I got acquainted with new people, that I had been taught many things which youths of my age did not commonly know: and that many persons would be disposed to talk to me of this and to compliment me upon it. What other things he said on this topic I remember very imperfectly, but he wound up by saying that whatever I knew more than others, could not be ascribed to any merit in me, but to the very unusual advantage which had fallen to my lot, of having a father who was able to teach me, and willing to give the necessary trouble and time; that it was no matter of praise to me, if I knew more than those who had not had a similar advantage, but the deepest disgrace to me if I did not.[2]

Norbert Wiener's father also took credit for his son's success:

> My father had reiterated that my success, if indeed, I had had any genuine success, was not so much a result of any superior ability on my part as of his training. This opinion he had expressed in print in various articles and interviews. He claimed that I was a most average boy who had been brought to a high level of accomplishment by the merit of his teaching and by that merit alone.[3]

While these examples are out of the ordinary, they do illustrate how parents focused upon creating a superkid can become enamored of their own Pygmalion-like powers. And it can be disastrous for a child when a parent, totally denying a child's efforts and abilities, takes credit for that child's exceptional achievements.

GOLD-MEDAL PARENTS

Another group of parents want their children to become Olympic-class athletes or competitors. Gold-Medal parents tend to be in routine middle-management positions with little hope for advancement, often not particularly involved in or committed to careers. They seek escape from the dull routine of uninteresting jobs or homemaking and child-rearing through their children's participation in sports or in other competitions. Gold-Medal parents are willing to invest a great deal of time and money in the children's training and competition. For example, parents who involve their children in ice skating have to pay for the coach, for rink time (which adds up when the child skates every day), for costumes as well as skates, and for transportation and hotel costs—not to mention time away from work—when the child competes at regional or national competitions. And driving a child to the rink early every morning and late every afternoon reflects the extent of parental commitment to the child's activity.

Gold-Medal parents have always had the "superkid" mentality, but contemporary parents of this stamp believe they have a better chance of creating a "star" if they start their children at the earliest possible age. Such parents are enrolling children at younger and younger ages in competitive activities without any real justification. Preschool children are being enrolled in swimming, gymnastics, skiing, and skating programs. More than a million infants and young children compete in preschool beauty contests. While there may be value in starting a talented youngster in athletics or other competitive activities after the age of seven or eight, there is little reason for starting a child before that age and certainly none at all for beginning before the age of five.

In the first place, the young child is put at risk physically. Because muscles do not attain full volume and bones are not totally calcified until adolescence, rigorous sports activities may do the child real physical harm. This is already happening to school-age youngsters who engage in relentless training in order to be number one.

The patient winced while taking off his jacket; excruciating pain stabbed at his shoulder.

A medical exam showed inflammation of the sac-shaped cavity filled with gluey fluids that lessens the friction between the tendons and the bony masses in the shoulder.

The diagnosis: Bursitis, a common ailment of aging.

But the patient, an avid swimmer, was only nine years old.

"He developed bursitis from sports," said Dr. Lyle Miticheli, director of the sports medicine clinic at Boston's Children's Hospital.

"Sports medicine physicians and clinics are seeing more children with adult diseases and injuries from sports and dance than in the past," says Miticheli. "It is not uncommon for children to develop tendinitis, knee injuries, torn cartilage, stress fractures of the spine, legs and long bones and to damage shoulders, elbows and growth plates."

Children's clinic sees an average of 150 sports-injured youngsters per week. In the past three years, partly because of the increased attention to sports medicine, the number of patients has grown from about 200 to 600 a month. Ninety percent of the children are injured in organized sports.[4]

There is also a psychological risk when children experience competition at too early an age, before they have the sense of security and self-esteem to handle it. Not everyone agrees, however, that the risks are all that bad. Mothers, for example, who enter their daughters in beauty contests argue that competition at an early age is beneficial for the child's personality development.

Mrs. Tony Hollingsworth of Rochester carefully stroked eye shadow and mascara on her 4 year old daughter Erica as she noted, "people don't realize how much time goes into these things, especially in the talent."

Mother and daughter were backstage at the Kids of America Pageant held one day recently at Stadium Junior High School in Abilene, Texas.

"She gets frustrated if she drops her baton or feels she doesn't do as good as she should," Mrs. Hollingsworth continued, as she brushed her daughter's blonde curls and put finishing touches on her makeup.

She smiled as she watched Erica go through her twirling routine, giving pointers—"Don't throw it as high on the stage. Don't get frustrated. Don't make faces if you drop it."—and she admitted with a laugh, "She's doing what I never had the guts to do. I'm living vicariously through my daughter: as long as I don't push her and she makes the decision whether she wants to be in the pageant.

"I think a lot of people misunderstand what these pageants are all about. They think that it's all just show and they're out there to show how pretty they are," Mrs. Hollingsworth added. "It [the pageant] teaches them discipline, self-control and how to win and lose gracefully."[5]

Even those who organize the pageants, however, recognize that potential gains are purchased at the expense of considerable risk.

"I do not like it when a mother gets angry and upset because her daughter doesn't win, or if the mother throws a tantrum and tells the judges off," says Jimmie Anne DeRoss, who is state director for the Texas Sunburst Pageant, and who mentioned as another of her pet peeves, "The pageant girls who go from pageant to pageant with their plastic smiles. I prefer a natural smile and natural responses."[6]

Gold-Medal parents who enter youngsters in athletic or other competitions before they are five are miseducating their children, putting them at risk for no purpose. Granted, some young children may learn something from the experience of being in a beauty contest or other type of competition at the age of four, but could they not learn the same thing in a less risky and more healthy (not to mention less expensive) way? A child in a good nursery school program would not only acquire self-confidence and self-esteem but acquire them in age-appropriate activities.

Nothing is lost and much is gained by postponing competitive activities until a child has at least attained the plateau of growth that occurs by the age of six or seven. The eruption of the permanent teeth is a good index of when the child is really ready for formal instruction and competition. To be sure, some parents who try to create superathletes from an early age succeed, but the number who fail is far, far greater, and the emotional—not to mention the financial—costs of failure can be catastrophic.

Do-It-Yourself Parents

Some parents have a back-to-nature bent and are concerned about the extent to which industry and technology are moving us away from our natural environment and our human nature. Many Do-It-Yourself parents live in cities but read magazines such as *The Mother Earth News* and dream about building a log cabin heated by a woodstove. Do-It-Yourself parents are often social and health service professionals, such as social workers, church administrators, and nurses, who tend to be relaxed in their child-rearing, allowing their children to develop at their own pace and in their own time.

Many Do-It-Yourself parents, who are increasingly dissatisfied with educational programs offered in the public schools, have, often unawares, become caught up in the "superkid" psychology as a way of protecting their child against the inadequacies of contemporary society. Without being fully aware of the fact, Do-It-Yourself parents want to create superkids who will be protective of the environment, of nature, and of animal life. Do-It-Yourself parents have also accepted the contemporary wisdom that to create a superkid, "earlier is better."

I met Mary and Michael J. at a La Leche League meeting in Washington, D.C., where I was giving a lecture. I had just checked into the hotel and was having a late lunch at the restaurant when Michael came over to my table and introduced himself, his wife, Mary, and their seven-month-old baby. They were from Tennessee, where Michael served as the youth minister of his church. Mary, a nurse who had taken time off to rear a family, asked me what I thought about home schooling. I told her that while I did not see it as the wave of the future (two-career couples and single parents are becoming more rather than less common, so there are fewer parents who are staying home with children and therefore fewer parents who might engage in home schooling), I thought it was a meaningful option for those parents who chose it, and I could see the potential risks as well as advantages.

Then Mary raised a question I had not expected. She said, "I don't plan to teach them at home once they reach school age, but I thought I might teach them to read while they are still toddlers so they will have a better chance once they get to school. I have a couple of books on teaching young children to read, and it looks pretty simple and straightforward."

Here was a "Do-It-Yourself" mother who had, I believe, unconsciously accepted the "superkid" psychology. Without being fully aware of it, she was expressing a desire to have a child who was beyond the norm. She and Michael were really not aware that they wanted a superkid and that this desire was in many ways a direct contradiction to their otherwise egalitarian and humanistic ethos. The presence of the "superkid" psychology in Do-It-Yourself parents speaks to its pervasiveness.

OUTWARD BOUND PARENTS

For some parents, the first educational priority is providing their children with the skills to survive in a hostile world. Many of these parents have been or are in the armed services or in professions such as law enforcement, while others are young professionals who are caught up in the fitness craze and see survival skills as a fringe benefit. Outward Bound parents are particularly aware of the dangers that confront children today—abduction of children from homes and stores, the sexual abuse of children by adult care-givers, and so on—and are introducing children to survival training at the infant and preschool level.

Outward Bound parents, like Do-It-Yourself parents, seem to have unwittingly accepted the "superkid" mentality. They want children who are exceptionally able to protect themselves from all dangers. Outward Bound parents, therefore, are particularly susceptible to those entrepreneurs who urge parents to put their babies into swimming classes so "they will not drown," or to enter preschool boys and girls in classes dealing with the martial arts so that they can "protect" themselves, or to purchase commercial programs that promise to teach children how to recognize and avoid "strangers" who might do them harm.

Unfortunately, Outward Bound parents have also tacitly accepted the proposition that the earlier you start a child in self-protection training, the more likely that child is to be above the norm in the ability to deal with trouble. When such training is extended downward to infants and young children, however, it becomes particularly dangerous, for two different but related reasons.

For one thing, the training of infants and young children in self-protection skills also involves a subtle shift of responsibility from parent to child. If our babies know how to swim, then we do not need to worry so much about their accidentally falling into the pool. If our children know about not going with strangers, then we need not be as concerned as we otherwise might be about keeping children out of potentially dangerous places. By teaching children survival skills, we may also be placing undue responsibility on our young children and reducing our own parental vigilance.

Second, current commercial programs aimed at helping parents teach their three- and four-year-olds to protect themselves against drowning or child abuse really don't work and should not be relied on. An infant who is taught to swim, for example, may lose that skill in a week, or a month, or a year. We cannot expect infants to retain skills as older children or adults do. In the same way, three- or four-year-olds cannot really protect themselves against adults who wish to do them harm. Children at this age are really not able to distinguish people who seem nice and mean them harm from people who seem nice and mean them well.

For example, a mother spent an hour with her four-year-old daughter explaining why she should not go with strangers. Finally the mother asked, "Do you understand, do you understand?" Her daughter replied, "Yes, yes, I understand, but what is a stranger?"

Another example: a four-year-old boy was told by his mother not to go into the backyard play area alone. One day the mother saw her son playing by himself in the yard, and she immediately went out and asked why he had gone outside alone. The child replied, "Oh, I will know the bad man when he comes, and I will run inside." The mother queried, "But how will you know the bad man?" "Oh," replied the child, "he will have a bandage on his head." "A bandage on his head?" asked the mother, perplexed. "Yes," answered her son, "didn't you say the bad man was sick in the head?"

It is our responsibility as parents to make every effort to ensure that the adults to whom we entrust our children's care are going to look out for our children's welfare. We cannot really educate young children to do this for themselves. Programs that encourage parents to instruct children in this way encourage a subtle and inappropriate shift of responsibility from parent to child and may lead parents into a dangerous sense of false security.

This does not mean that we should not say anything to young children about not going with strangers; it does mean that we should not expect young children to appreciate the message fully until they are six or seven. Likewise, if swimming and exercise classes for young children provide a social outing for the parents and are developmentally appropriate for the child, the physical risks are reduced and balanced by the healthy interaction such activities promote between parent and child. On the other hand, if such programs are sold on the basis of teaching young children survival skills, they amount to miseducation. When we shift our parental responsibilities onto our children, we put them at risk to no purpose.

PRODIGY PARENTS

Prodigy parents are often couples who have become financially successful but not through the usual channels of education. With little more, and in many cases less, than a high school education, they have built a successful business and, not surprisingly, have mixed feelings about education and about "intellectuals." They did not enjoy their own education and have a certain distrust of things academic in general and of intellectuals in particular. On the other hand, they feel an attraction for the "class" an education provides, namely, the language and manners of the educated. Prodigy parents expect their children to "go into the business," but want them to bring a "touch of class" along with them.

The "superkid" psychology has considerable appeal for Prodigy parents because many feel that they themselves were prodigies (self-made superkids, if you will) of a sort, that they were successful because of a special talent or ability, not because of schooling, and they tend to see education as a force for dulling and blunting this ability. Not surprisingly, Prodigy parents see their children as prodigies, too, and worry about the price their children will have to pay for the "class" of education. The "earlier is better" idea is appealing, for it suggests that there is something parents can do to help their children acquire the "class" before being exposed to the debilitating experience of school.

Accordingly, Prodigy parents are attracted to those writers and books (such as Glenn Doman's *Teach Your Baby to Read* and *Teach Your Baby Math* or Siegfried and Therese Engelmann's *Give Your Child a Superior Mind* or Sidney Ledson's *Teach Your Child to Read in Sixty Days*) which suggest that the schools are doing a poor job and that the child's talents and abilities are being underdeveloped and stunted. These writers promise Prodigy parents that their children can be safeguarded against the negative effects of schooling while retaining the "class." It is not accidental that these programs often offer "classy subjects" such as foreign language and music instruction as well as reading and math.

Some Prodigy parents can make a strong case. After a recent lecture in which I talked about some of the risks of early instruction, an irate mother approached me. "I think that some of the things you said were dead wrong. My son is four now, and he reads at the fourth-grade level, he speaks Japanese, and he plays the violin very well. He is also a healthy, happy little boy. So what is wrong with that? Look at all the advantages he has, and how far ahead he is of his peers. Would I have done him a better service if I simply wasted these precious years and let him play and watch television?"

I congratulated this mother on her dedication and on her success. I reiterated what I have said in my books and in the lecture, namely, that early instruction has its risks. Apparently, her child was fortunate and escaped the immediate risks—of frustration, failure, and undue identification of academic accomplishment with self-worth. But even the accomplished child has problems. Parents like this mother, I am sure, are tempted not only to boast about their children but also to put them on display. One four-year-old I knew broke into tears every time his mother insisted he play the violin for guests.

And the child who escapes some of the dangers of early instruction may suffer some of the risks of being different from peers. Not the least of these risks is the possibility of being heartily disliked by age mates. A teacher told me of one such child who was constantly showing off and telling her what she was doing wrong! Being a mass-produced prodigy can be a pain, to other people at least.

The real problem with fabricated prodigies is that the trappings of a liberal arts education are simply unsuited to the demeanor of young children. A true liberal arts education is the capstone of general education, not its foundation. In a young child, the pretension to sophistication in language, music, math, and the arts seems even a little monstrous. It denies the true nature of young children—how far they have to go before they attain genuine intellectual sophistication—and is a vulgarization of a true liberal arts education. Unfortunately, many parents who wish to produce prodigies, end up by producing parodies.

Encounter Group Parents

Some parents are very caught up in the latest therapies and psychological fads. Often they are college-educated professionals or business people who may not have done as well financially as their parents. More often than not they have been in therapy either as a child or as an adult. Encounter Group parents are very committed to honesty, to "up-frontness," to "communication," to "connecting," and to "networking" or to whatever new catchwords are in vogue. Although Encounter Group parents are less common today than a decade ago, they are still extant, particularly in urban areas. Many Encounter Group parents are divorced singles or in a second marriage and are particularly sensitive to the stress of separation and loss.

These parents value relationships and work to maintain and preserve relationships; when all of the trendy language and techniques are put aside, that is their real strength. But Encounter Group parents, no less than the other parental types described above, have also unconsciously assimilated the "superkid" psychology. Without being fully aware of it, I believe, Encounter Group parents want children who are exceptionally psychologically sensitive and perceptive. They want "psychological" superkids.

Encounter Group parents have also assimilated the idea that to produce a superkid, of any variety, "earlier is better." As a consequence, Encounter Group parents have come to believe that it is never too early to tell children about death, about the dangers of nuclear war and of the potential abductor and molester; that it is healthy for young children to see parents nude. This can sometimes backfire. An Encounter Group couple were entertaining some friends, and one couple had

47

brought their baby boy. When the mother went to change the baby, the three-year-old daughter of the hosts went along. When they returned, the little girl announced to the company, "My daddy's is much bigger than his!"

Unfortunately, Encounter Group parents may get caught up in child-rearing fads that have little or no basis in cultural, social, or religious tradition or in child-development research and theory. Having children witness the birth of siblings is a case in point. A quite obviously pregnant mother approached me after a recent lecture and asked what I thought of her having her four-year-old son witness the birthing of her forthcoming child. The question caught me off guard and I resorted to the psychologist's strategy of answering a question with a question when one doesn't have a ready answer. So I said, "Why would you want to do that [adding, under my breath: "for goodness sake!"]?" To which she replied, "It will bring us closer together as a family."

I thought about that for a moment and said, "It seems to me that an experience of that kind might be quite frightening for a four-year-old, and I would be happy to suggest some less violent ways that might bring you closer together as a family." At that moment another mother who had overheard the conversation came into the discussion. "Oh, don't listen to him," she said. "I had my two-year-old son witness the birthing of his brother, and he is six now and he is still talking about it!" When I told this story at another lecture, a mother came up to me afterward and said, "I didn't have my son witness the birthing, but he did wash the baby and cut the cord!" And then she said with some disappointment, "He is eleven now and she is six, and they still fight."

There is a time and a place for everything, and early childhood is not the time to tell children about nuclear war or about death or to have them witness the facts of life. I say this not from some romantic notion of childhood "innocence" but rather because of some hard-headed facts about child development.

Young children do not have the concepts to understand death, much less birth. For children before the age of eight or nine, death is simply a going away, while birth is simply coming back. Witnessing a birthing for a child is witnessing a painful, bloody, and incomprehensible event that is unrelated to pro-creation, gestation, and the like. As such, it is a frightening experience for a young child, with little that is redeeming or constructive to balance its negative impact.

To be sure, when the child is witness to such events by chance, we need to deal with them directly and openly; it is important to talk and encourage the child to express the feel-ings he or she might have about the experience. Even hearing about matters of life and death can be frightening. A patient of mine, a nine-year-old girl, had an anxiety attack some two weeks after the baby of a friend of her mother's died of sudden infant death syndrome. Before she had a chance to talk about her feelings, fears and anxieties emerged in a sudden burst of uncontrollable crying.

Deliberate early exposure of a child to emotional events does not ensure a psychological superkid. In fact, the result may be just the opposite—an emotionally troubled youngster.

MILK-AND-COOKIES PARENTS

Not all parents today have succumbed consciously or uncon-sciously to the "superkid" psychology. Many of us want our children to work hard and be successful but also to enjoy their childhood, to prepare for the future but also to enjoy the unique joys and stresses of each stage of life. Most Milk-and-Cookies parents have had a happy childhood, which they recall with pleasure and which they want their children to have as well. I find Milk-and-Cookies parents in all occupations and at all social levels. What they have in common is a genuine reverence for childhood as a stage of life which is just as valuable as any other and which must be preserved.

Milk-and-Cookies parents tend to have a relaxed attitude toward their children. For example, they see the baby as young and relatively helpless and in need of care and attention. While they take pleasure and pride in the baby's achievements, such as smiling and standing with support, they have no inclination to rush the child through a developmental timetable. Milk-and-Cookies parents are often filled with wonder at their baby, at the successive miracles of growth and development. They become naturalists of sorts, observing the child's progress with pleasure and amazement.

This is how one Milk-and-Cookies father described coming home to his infant daughter after a brief trip:

> I rode back to Columbus and went straight to Susan's parents' house, where Susan and Amanda were staying. I rang the bell and Susan opened it with Amanda in her arms.
>
> "Remember me?" I said to Amanda.
>
> Her face lit up. She grinned and bobbed her head and started to move towards me.
>
> "It's amazing," Susan's mother said. "She really hasn't done that for anyone else. She really knows who you are."
>
> I don't know whether to believe that or not. She's still so little—and Susan and I always tell ourselves that she can't possibly know us, even with all the time we spend with her.
>
> But the look in her eye, and her reaction to me, convinced me that she really might know. Can it be true? I go away for two days and when I come back she knows that I'm her father?
>
> I hope so.[7]

As a rule, Milk-and-Cookies parents are not inclined to miseducation. Nonetheless, the pervasiveness of the "super-kid" psychology in contemporary society puts a lot of pressure on Milk-and-Cookies parents. When other parents are putting their babies in gym and exercise classes, Milk-and-Cookies parents begin to wonder whether they are depriving their babies of important experiences, to wonder whether the "superbabies" in these various programs will have some kind of an edge over their own children.

Despite these considerations, most Milk-and-Cookies parents resist the pressures and provide a secure, warm, stimulating environment. They have the feeling that if children are well cared for, are talked to, played with, and provided with a safe environment filled with interesting objects to observe and explore, they will do just fine. And these parents are right. The child who leaves the early years with a strong sense of security, a healthy feeling of self-esteem, and an enthusiasm for living and learning is well prepared for an admittedly rapidly changing and difficult world.

It is important to reiterate that the parenting styles described here are not mutually exclusive: there is more than a little of each style in every one of us. And each of these parenting styles can be the basis for healthy child-rearing and education. The risks arise when we get caught up in the "superkid" psychology and try to produce a superkid by imposing a life-style too early, before the child is ready to cope with our adult trappings and exertions. In the end, if we only take the time and make the effort to appreciate our children on their own terms, we will discover that every child is indeed a super kid.

3

The Competent Child: Miseducation in the Schools

THE CHILD IS a gift of nature, but the image of the child is mankind's creation. During any historical period, the image of the child that dictates educational practice is more reflective of the prevailing Zeitgeist than it is of established wisdom regarding what is good pedagogy for children. A case in point is the contemporary image of the competent child that originated in the social upheavals of the 1960s, and accounts for much of the miseducation of young children in our schools today.

Our earlier religious image of the "sinful" child was replaced during the 1930s and '40s with the Freudian concept of the "sensual" child, abrim with sexual feelings whose epicenter moved from the mouth to the anus and finally to the genital region by the age of four or five. Freud argued that pleasure-seeking actions of the infant and young child (such as thumb-sucking and masturbation) were normal expressions of these stages of psychosexual development.

The image of the sensual child took hold in the middle decades of this century because it both supported and reinforced major changes then occurring in our society. Particularly after the Second World War, as defense plants closed and as other jobs were needed for returning servicemen, working women were told, often by professionals writing in popular magazines, that "maternal deprivation" was bad for their infants and young children. John Bowlby, in a most influential early-1950s book entitled *Child Care and the Growth of Love*, warned mothers:

> The absolute need of infants and toddlers for the continuous care of their mothers will be borne in on all who read this book. . . . We must recognize that leaving any child under three years of age is a major operation only to be undertaken with good and sufficient reasons and, when undertaken, to be planned with great care.[1]

Bowlby exaggerated his case, perhaps because he was influenced by the social dynamics of his times, just as the writers described below exaggerated theirs in response to a new set of social circumstances. The upshot was that the concept of "maternal deprivation" reinforced the image of the sensual child and provided a convenient rationale for getting and keeping middle-class women out of the work force. In addition, with the availability of inexpensive automobiles after the war, America became rapidly suburbanized. The image of the sensual child who needed not only continuous maternal attention but also a backyard to play in (to express himself or herself, in order to avoid neurosis later) also provided a rationale for suburban family life.

During the reign of the sensual child, little attention was paid to the child's intellectual abilities, which were assumed to receive their optimum stimulation in a relaxed, unrepressed urban setting.

The concept of a sensual child was epitomized in the work of Benjamin Spock, a pediatrician who had almost become a psychoanalyst. His book *Infant and Child Care*, first published in 1946, combined solid pediatric advice with a Freudian-influenced understanding of children's emotional development. In the first edition of the book, Spock took for granted that mothers would stay home to take care of their infants and young children.

The sensual child was largely a middle-class conception. Low-income parents could not purchase homes in the suburbs, and many low-income mothers could not afford to give up work to stay home and care for their children during the first three years. Low-income parents could not afford the luxury of the sensual child or the psychology of maternal deprivation. Among these parents, and particularly among immigrant parents, whose children had to serve as mediators of the new culture to their parents, there was a concept of childhood "competence." But while low-income parents assumed that their children were competent to take on age-appropriate, or more than age-appropriate, social responsibilities, they did not expect their children to master academics at an early age.

Psychologists had not previously studied low-income children, but in the 1960s, with the civil rights movement and the War on Poverty focusing attention on low-income children, professionals rediscovered the concept of competence. Infants and young children, we were told, had greater intellectual powers than we had been led to believe, and early stimulation was necessary for a realization of those powers. Lewis P. Lipsitt, an outstanding infant researcher at Brown University, in a 1971 article entitled "Babies Are a Lot Smarter Than They Look," wrote:

> Are we prepared to provide presumably beneficial educational experiences to children at much younger age levels than we do, particularly if such experiences are discovered to be critical to laying down lifelong learning styles?[2]

If "disadvantaged" children had low IQs and were doing poorly in school, it was because they had been deprived of appropriate intellectual stimulation. Early-childhood programs, such as nursery school, regarded as a frill for middle-class children, came to be seen as a "must" for low-income children if their competence was to be realized and if the cycle of poverty was ever to be interrupted.

The concept of infant and young-child competence was, of course, not original with psychologists of the 1960s and '70s. In the 1920s, psychologist John Watson espoused a concept of infant "malleability" that is a central component of the competence concept: if infants and young children are able learners, they can also be "shaped" by their early learning. Watson wrote:

> Give me a dozen healthy infants, well formed, and my own special world to bring them up in, and I'll guarantee you to take any one at random and train him to become any type of specialist I might select—doctor, lawyer, artist, merchant chief, and yes, even beggar and thief, regardless of his talents, penchants, tendencies, vocations, and race of his ancestors.[3]

Watson's audience was not ready for the competent child; the idea of the "sensual" child was much better suited to the family-oriented middle-class life-styles of the decades from the twenties to the sixties.

But the notion of the competent child, introduced to remedy the plight of disadvantaged children, has come to dominate the thinking of middle-class educators and parents in the 1980s; it just happens to be in keeping with contemporary middle-class life-styles. Unfortunately, the image of unrealized child competence is as much an exaggeration as the previous image of the child as a potential victim of maternal deprivation.

The conception of the competent child was spearheaded

by professionals who, like Bowlby before them, were responding more to the social and political climate of the times than they were to "new" research findings. Psychologists in the sixties proclaimed that the mental capacities and learning abilities of young children had been seriously underestimated. Educators, in turn, began to argue that academic instruction in the early years was critical for later academic learning. The mental testers argued that the IQ was not fixed at birth and could be significantly changed by the right stimulation in infancy and early childhood. And social historians, who adopted childhood as a new area of research, were arguing that childhood and adolescence were social "inventions" and that age differences recognized today were unheard of in the Middle Ages.

All of these ideas, made available to parents by articles in the popular press, emphasized not only child competence but also the importance of what came to be called "early intervention." In addition, at universities all over the country, research programs were undertaken to demonstrate in a scientific way the efficacy of early-childhood intervention for low-income children. A communication network, ERIC (Early Childhood Resource and Information Center), was set up to disseminate the findings from the different early-childhood education programs.

The social reformers of the 1960s did not think they were tampering with the middle-class concept of the "sensual" child when they heralded the "competence" of low-income children. They wanted to give low-income children a chance and often went somewhat beyond what the data warranted in order to make their point. The concept of the competent infant and young child, then, was rediscovered in the context of social reform and in a spirit of social responsibility. And it was taken over by middle-class educators and parents, not because of any revolutionary findings or theories, but because the image of the competent child is better suited than the image of the sensual child to the pressures on contemporary educators and the life-styles of contemporary parents.

We need to look now at four pivotal ideas introduced in the 1960s that were aimed primarily at lower-income children, and at how they have been inappropriately extended and distorted when applied to middle-income children both at home and at school. The superkid psychology described in the last chapter is one such distorted derivative, and formal instruction of young children in the schools is another. In a way, this discussion provides a case study of how overzealous educational theory can support miseducation.

THE COMPETENT CHILD OF THE 1960S

Competence as Unlimited Learning Ability

One of the most influential contributors to the concept of the competent child was then Harvard psychologist Jerome Bruner. In 1960 Bruner published *The Process of Education*, which was a best seller and became something of a bible for the curriculum reform movement of the sixties. At that time we were deeply embarrassed that the Russians had launched the first manned space vehicle (the Sputnik, in 1957) and we were determined to improve our science and math education. Of particular importance to us here is a hypothesis which Bruner proposed and which has become one of the maxims of the competent child concept: "We begin with the hypothesis that any subject can be taught effectively in some intellectually honest way to any child at any stage of development."[4]

Bruner was not writing about children so much as about curriculum: he wanted curriculum writers to devise reading, math, and science curricula that could be taught to young children. If children could be started in these subjects at an early age, presumably they would be more proficient than if they started later. The real challenge was to find ways of translating difficult subject matter into concepts and skills that could be learned by young children.*

But some educators interpreted Bruner's hypothesis about curriculum and instruction to be a hypothesis about learning. That is to say, they interpreted it to mean, not that children could be "taught" anything at any age, but rather that children could "learn" anything at any age. The difference is important. We can change the level of the content and the methods we use to instruct children, but we cannot change the ways in which children learn. To say that a child can learn anything at any age ignores all that we know about the growth and development of children.

A personal example may help to illustrate this difference between our ability to change the level of instruction without affecting the child's ability to learn. When my son Robert was four, he came into my study one day and said, "Daddy, I can tell time." Knowing as I did that children are usually not able to read a clockface until the age of six or seven, I thought it was an empty boast. Nonetheless, I asked, "Oh, what time is it?" To this Bobby answered, "It is eleven-thirty." I looked at my watch and was surprised to discover that he was right.

"How did you do that?" I asked. Bobby replied, "I told you, I can tell time." It occurred to me that Bobby had been experimenting with the telephone and that perhaps he had discovered how to dial for time and temperature. So I asked, "Did you call up for the time?" Bobby responded with some exasperation, "No, Daddy, I told you I could tell time—come watch me." At that point he took me by the hand and led me to our bedroom, where there was a digital clock-radio. Bobby was reading the time from a digital clock!

A digital clock makes the task of telling time much easier

*Bruner believes that his hypothesis has never really been refuted, but also that it has been widely misunderstood. With respect to young children he told me, "You have to be exquisitely and constantly aware of where the child is so as to adapt your materials to the levels and limits of the child's understanding."

than telling time from a clockface. Telling time from a clockface requires an understanding that one and the same number, and place, can stand for three different things. The number and place on a clockface of the "three," for example, can mean three hours, fifteen minutes, or fifteen seconds. But on a digital clock, hours, minutes, and seconds each have a different place. A digital clock removes some of the logical difficulties in telling time from a traditional clockface. Despite his discovery, Bobby, like most children, was not able to tell time from a regular clock or watch until he was seven.

Just as a child's ability to read a digital clock does not mean that he can learn to tell time from a clockface, so, in the same way, a child's ability to learn a few words from sight does not mean that he or she can learn phonics. Yet the Bruner hypothesis has been interpreted to mean just that, that a child can learn any level of subject matter at any age. It is just that misinterpretation which lies behind much of the miseducation practiced in the schools today.

When the first-grade curriculum is pushed down into the kindergarten and the kindergarten curriculum is taught to four-year-olds, as is happening in too many programs for four-year-olds, we see the results of this false concept of young children's competence. Young children learn in a different manner from that of older children and adults, yet we can teach them many things if we adapt our materials and mode of instruction to their level of ability. But we miseducate young children when we assume that their learning abilities are comparable to those of older children and that they can be taught with materials and with the same instructional procedures appropriate to school-age children.

Competence as Readiness to Learn

Another writer who contributed to the new image of the competent child was University of Chicago educational psychologist Benjamin Bloom, who in his 1964 book *Stability and Change in Human Characteristics* examined changes in IQ and achievement scores from the preschool years through high school. On the basis of his statistical analysis Bloom argued in this book that intellectual growth is very rapid during the preschool years: "General intelligence appears to develop as much from conception to age four as it does during the fourteen years from age four to eighteen."[5]

Inasmuch as intellectual development as measured by IQ tests reaches a peak at age eighteen, Bloom's statement has been widely taken to mean that a child attains half of his or her intellectual potential by the age of four. A corollary to that proposition was Bloom's contention that "the environment would have its greatest effect upon a characteristic (i.e., a trait like intelligence) during its most rapid development."[6]

Taken together, these two ideas reinforced the image of child competence derived from the misinterpretation of Bruner's hypothesis—the notion that young children not only are more able learners than we have given them credit for being, but are also better learners than they will be later. Bloom's conclusions gave great impetus to the importance of education in general and formal instruction in particular during the early years. Although these ideas were meant to underscore the need to provide early-childhood education for disadvantaged children of the sixties, they have been widely assimilated into the image of child competence held by educators and middle-class parents today.

We need, however, to reexamine those conclusions, which provided such a powerful rationale for educational reform two decades ago and for the miseducation so common today. (Please understand, I am not accusing Bruner or Bloom of pandering to the demands of the times. But, whether lay persons or professionals, we are alike products of our social environment, and scientists can get as caught up in the spirit of social movements as anyone else. At such times a bias, however unconscious, favors conclusions that fit with and support the direction of social change.)

In the first place, what does it mean when Benjamin Bloom says that children attain half of their intellectual potential by the age of four? Does it mean that children have experienced half of all they will ever experience? Obviously not. Does it mean that children have attained half of all the information they will ever acquire? Improbable. Does it mean that children will have attained half of all the intellectual skills they will ever master? Not likely. Does it mean that at four the child with an IQ of 50 will eventually end up with an IQ of 100? Obviously not.

So what does it really mean? First of all, the data upon which Bloom based his conclusions was not new and had been around for decades. The data consists of studies that attempt to assess the accuracy with which we can predict a child's IQ from one testing to another. In the field of mental testing there are two basic concepts. One is validity, the extent to which a test measures what it is supposed to measure. If a test is supposed to measure intelligence, for example, and a person who scores at the mental-defective level makes an outstanding scientific discovery, this does not speak well for the validity of the test. The other concept is reliability, the extent to which test scores are consistent from testing to testing. If a child scores 100 on an IQ test at one time and 150 a few weeks later—without any obvious changes in the child's life circumstances—the test cannot be said to be reliable.

One of the best-established findings in the mental-testing field is that infant tests are neither valid nor reliable indices of performance on intelligence tests at later ages. Perhaps the major reason for this discrepancy is that most intelligence tests for older children, adolescents, and adults are heavily verbal in both instructions and task content. Infant tests, in contrast, most often involve motor performance.

But even after young children begin to talk (at ages two

and three) and are able to respond to verbal IQ test items, their performance is still not a good predictor of later IQ test attainments. Young children are not test-conscious and are not concerned about doing well. Their performance will vary with their mood, how they feel about the testing, what else has happened to them that day, and so on. It is difficult, then, on the basis of an IQ test given to young children to assess what the child's real IQ is and how the child will score at a later date.

By the age of four, however, children have become more socialized and their attention span is longer. They are more interested in their performance on a test and are more concerned with doing well than they were as infants and toddlers. Accordingly, the IQ test scores of four-year-old children are a better predictor of children's true intelligence and of their test intelligence at a later point in life than it was at age two or age three. With the aid of statistical procedures, it is possible to measure the accuracy with which we can predict the IQ score an individual will attain at a later age from the one attained at an earlier age.

It has been shown that, using these procedures, you can predict with 50 percent accuracy, from an IQ score attained at age four, what that child's IQ score will be when he or she is retested at the age of eighteen. In addition, if you plot the accuracy of prediction against age, you attain a curve that rises rapidly in early childhood and becomes flat at about the age of eighteen. What this curve means is that the shorter the times between test and retest, the more reliable the attained test scores. Yet that curve has been described as a curve of "mental growth," which is said to mirror the rate at which children attain knowledge, skills, and abilities!

So when Bloom argued that children attained half of their intellectual ability by age four and that mental growth was more rapid in the early years, he was basing his conclusions on test scores and statistics, not upon the vast body of research on how children grow and learn. Even the most cursory examination of the literature on child development would give the lie to the idea that children attain half of their intellectual prowess by age four. Bärbel Inhelder and Jean Piaget have shown, for example, that not until adolescence do young people attain the mental abilities necessary to engage in scientific experimentation, high-level mathematics, literary exegesis, and historical investigation. Nonetheless, Bloom's interpretations of the mental test data went unchallenged and were widely heralded by professionals as demonstrating the importance of formal instruction during the early years.*

It must be said that Bloom's interpretations were uncritically accepted, in part at least, because they got public education off a very sharp hook. In the 1960s the public schools were under attack for not being sufficiently rigorous and for not providing quality education for minorities. It was in this context that the Bloom report found a most welcome audience. If children did not do well in science and math, it was held, it was because of inadequate preparation at the preschool level. Likewise, if disadvantaged youngsters did poorly in public school, it was not necessarily because of the poor quality of public school education, but rather because the children came to school poorly prepared. Bloom's argument for the competence of young children and the critical importance of early-childhood education for later academic achievement provided a convenient and scientifically credible excuse for the poor academic achievement of American public school children.

---

*Although Bloom still regards the early years as critical for learning, he deplores those who interpret this to mean learning the three R's:

> What seems to me to be the most misdirected effort is the attempt by some parents and some preschool programs to teach children to read, write and do simple arithmetic in the nursery school and kindergarten. . . . What I do believe is that the learning experiences of these critical years should be directed to more important goals. These are the years when children should "learn to learn" rather than learn the particular skills usually taught in the first or the second grade. . . . That it is good for children to learn to read at ages 6 and 7 does not mean that it is better to learn this skill at younger ages. I do not think we can justify taking over the precious years of childhood to give children an early start in the three r's.[7]

Competence as IQ Malleability

Still another contribution to the image of the competent infant was provided by University of Illinois psychologist J. McV. Hunt. In 1961 Hunt published a book entitled *Intelligence and Experience*, in which he critically examined the concept of the "fixed" IQ. Hunt correctly pointed out that the notion of a fixed, unalterable IQ held by some practitioners had led to many educational reforms as well as abuses. The recognition that some children could not learn because of limited mental ability rather than laziness or moral corruption led to more humane educational practices. On the other hand, the idea that intelligence was, for the most part, fixed at birth implied that there was little if any purpose to trying to improve it by stimulation and cultivation.

After a comprehensive survey of the literature of the time, including animal research, work with computers, and the research of Jean Piaget, Hunt concluded:

> In the light of these considerations, it appears that the counsel from experts on child rearing during the third and much of the fourth decades of the twentieth century to let children be while they grow and to avoid excessive stimulation was highly unfortunate. . . . It is no longer unreasonable to consider that it might be feasible to discover ways to govern encounters children have with their environments, especially during the early years of development, to achieve a substantially faster rate of mental development and a substantially higher adult level of intellectual capacity.[8]

Hence young children not only are able (Bruner) and ready (Bloom) learners but also have malleable IQs that can be increased with appropriate early stimulation. Hunt thus elaborated the image of the competent infant in still another direction. Hunt's argument, like Bloom's, was directed primarily at the disadvantaged child who had an impoverished intellectual and cultural background. He drew his examples of the effectiveness of early stimulation from studies of orphans and from his own studies of abandoned infants in Iran.

But we need to examine Hunt's argument a bit more closely. In order to make his point about the malleability of the IQ, Hunt created something of a straw man, drawing a portrait of professionals who argued for the constancy of the IQ in a dogmatic way. In fact, of course, no responsible psychologist writing in the early decades of this century ever asserted that the IQ was absolutely constant. It was generally recognized that from 20 to 40 percent of the IQ is contributed by the environment. For example, Florence Goodenough, in her chapter, "The Measurement of Mental Growth in Children," in the authoritative *Manual of Child Psychology* (1954) had this to say about modifiability:

> That children reared from infancy in environments where intellectual opportunity is not lacking and where the incentive to intellectual achievement is high are likely to reach a higher level of achievement than others of equal original endowment for whom both opportunity and incentives are poor is conceded by practically all who have considered the matter.[9]

The failure of most psychologists to stress IQ modifiability has a simple explanation. Most of the research in the first half of this century was with middle-class children, who were readily available in nursery schools and university lab schools. Middle-class children, it was assumed, in keeping with the image of the sensual infant, lived in optimum environments for the realization of their intellectual potential. For such children, the idea that a considerable proportion of the IQ was determined by the environment has little significance, inasmuch as a changed environment would not be expected to be much of an improvement over the one they were currently experiencing.

But when the concept of IQ malleability was applied to disadvantaged children, presumably deprived of adequate intellectual stimulation, it took on great public policy significance. If these children were given more intellectual stimulation, were in the right educational program, their heretofore unused potential could be realized. At last we might be able to end the cycle of poverty and distress of low-income families. Hunt thus added another powerful argument for the notion of the competent infant and for the value of early intellectual stimulation and enrichment.

Competence as Hidden Potential

A final component of the image of the competent child came from a somewhat unexpected quarter—namely, social history. This contribution was made by the French historian Philippe Aries, whose book *Centuries of Childhood* was widely touted by the psychologists of the 1960s as providing another kind of evidence for their contention that infants and young children were more capable than they had been given credit for being. According to Aries, the concept of childhood as a separate stage of life, of children as different from adults in their levels of social and intellectual understanding, emerged only in the last four hundred years, and prior to the modern era children were treated much like adults.

In support of his thesis, Aries used documents and paintings of the times depicting children in adult dress and postures and a variety of written sources which seemed to suggest that adults treated children as equals. Young children, for example, performed many of the rituals and services now regarded as the province of adults:

> The youngest child takes a glass of wine in his right hand, together with some bread crumbs and a pinch of salt, while in his left hand he holds a lighted taper. All heads are bared and the child begins to intone the sign of the cross. In the name of the Father . . . he drops a pinch of salt at one end of the hearth . . . and so on. The embers, which are supposed to have a beneficial quality, are preserved after the ceremony.
>
> He [the child] played a like role on occasions which were less exceptional but which at the time possessed the same social character: family meals. It was traditional for grace to be said by one of the youngest children and for the meal to be served by all the children present: they poured out the drinks, changed the dishes, carved the meat.[10]

The idea of childhood as a social invention, argued by a number of social historians in addition to Aries (e.g., John Demos and Leonard DeMaus) had several implications that lent support to the image of the competent child. For one thing, Aries gave a historical account of how the competent child of the Middle Ages was transformed, for social reasons, into the innocent, helpless infant of the twentieth century. Thus, from a historical point of view, the contemporary concept of childhood exaggerates children's limitations and minimizes their competence. This dovetails nicely with the idea that young children are more able, ready, and malleable learners than they are given credit for being—the thrust of the child competence argument. Second, if childhood innocence and helplessness were social inventions, they could be disinvented. This implication directly supported the early-intervention strategies of the 1960s.

A number of contemporary social historians, however, have challenged the Aries thesis. Linda A. Pollock, for example, after an exhaustive study of diaries and autobiographies of parents writing from 1500 to 1900, concludes:

> The results of this study . . . demonstrate that the main arguments put forward by many historians are incorrect —they are at best only applicable to a minority of parents and children. Contrary to the belief of such authors as Aries, there was a concept of childhood in the 16th century. This may have become more elaborated through the centuries but, nonetheless, the 16th-century writers studied did appreciate that children were different from adults and were also aware of the ways in which children were different—the latter passed through certain recognizable developmental stages; they played; they required discipline, education and protection.[11]

The idea of childhood as a social invention, in retrospect, is hardly credible. In the Bible, in the writings of the Greeks and Romans, and in the works of the first great educator of the modern era, Comenius, children were recognized as being both different from adults and different from one another with respect to their stages of development. To be sure, the scientific study of children and the increased length of life in modern times have enhanced our understanding of age differences, but they have always been acknowledged. The ready acceptance of the idea of childhood and adolescence as social inventions in the 1960s has to be attributed, in large part, to the fact that it provided a different kind of evidence in favor of the image of the competent child being advocated by the social and educational reformers.

The image of child competence that emerged in the 1960s thus included the ideas that young children: could learn anything at any age; were more ready and able to learn than they would be at any later age; could raise their IQs with the right stimulation; and were being prevented from demonstrating their potential by a socially imposed persona of innocence. This new image was a powerful force for progressive social policy. Advocates of the competent child convinced Congress to pass the Head Start legislation in 1964, which by 1965 provided comprehensive education and health care to more than half a million disadvantaged youngsters. Legislation for "mainstreaming" children with special needs was another response to this new image. When it was taken over by middle-class parents and educators, however, the image of child competence became something altogether different.

THE CONCEPT OF CHILD COMPETENCE TODAY

The image of child competence introduced in the 1960s was intended to remedy some of the social inequalities visited upon low-income children. But the publicity given the arguments of child competence was read and heard by educators and middle-class parents as well. And the image of child competence was much more in keeping with the changing life-styles of middle-class families in the seventies and particularly in the eighties than was the concept of the sensual child. For this reason it was uncritically appropriated for middle-class children by parents and educators. While the image of childhood competence has served a useful function for low-income children and children with special needs, it has become the rationale for the miseducation of middle-class children both at home and at school.

Schools are once more under attack for not adequately preparing children academically. Particularly devastating are reports comparing the academic achievement of American children with those of other countries, such as Japan.[12] Educators are under pressure for accountability, for effectiveness, but most of all for improving the academic performance of the children in our schools. Longer hours, longer school years, more homework have all been proposed. But, in practice, what has been most implemented is the pushing of academics into the kindergarten and making kindergarten available for four-year-olds. While there are many reasons for these practices, one of them, even if unacknowledged, is the hope that starting children earlier in academics will improve their performance later.

Parents, also caught up in the fallacious image of early-childhood competence, have added to the pressure on schools to "go academic" at an early age. Today's parents give credence to the image of early-childhood competence often for unconscious but nonetheless quite powerful motives. Middle-class family configurations are very different today than they were in the past; there is more divorce, single parenting, blended families, two-career couples, and more need for the care of children outside of the home from an early age. But even liberated middle-class parents question what is best for their children and at how young an age (Bowlby's threat of maternal deprivation dies hard!). It takes away some of the guilt and uncertainty if we rationalize that in order to reach their full potential, young children need a great deal of intellectual stimulation, which can be provided only by academically oriented full-day early-childhood programs.

Accordingly, the image of the competent child introduced to remedy the understimulation of low-income children now serves as a rationale for the overstimulation of middle-class children. The reason why this constitutes miseducation is illustrated by the following analogy. If we have a group of undernourished children who are below the norm for height and weight and put them on a full-calorie, well-balanced diet, we will witness a remarkable improvement. The children will make substantial progress in height and weight. On the other hand, if we put a group of already well-nourished children on a full-calorie, well-balanced diet in addition to the one that they are already on, this will be detrimental to their health.

Please understand, I am not saying that the early years are unimportant for later intellectual ability and academic performance—far from it. I am saying that the image of the competent young child has caused a lot of confusion about what is healthy education for young children. It is essential that contemporary educators and parents separate the need to work and to have out-of-home care for our children from ideas about the critical importance of the early years. They are really two quite separate issues.

If we want and/or need to work when our children are small, we should accept this and be honest with ourselves and with our children. The bulk of the evidence suggests that young children who are cared for in high-quality programs suffer no untoward harm and can even benefit in significant ways. Once we accept this, we can devote our energies to encouraging the schools to provide programs that best fit the needs of our children instead of programs which offer relief from our guilt by falsely promising to raise our children's IQs or to make them more academically successful than they would be if formal instruction were begun later.

Early childhood is a very important period of life. It is a period when children learn an enormous amount about the everyday world. It is also the time during which young children acquire lifelong attitudes toward themselves, toward others, and toward learning. But it is not the time for formal academic instruction. To appreciate this truth, we need to see the early years for what they are and not through the lenses of social, political, and personal dynamics that provide a distorted image of early-childhood competence.

4

Status, Competition, and Computers: Miseducation as a Response to Social Pressure

HUMAN BEHAVIOR, Freud observed, is always over-determined, and miseducation is no exception to that rule. In addition to the "superkid" psychology that contributes to miseducation by some parents and the image of the "competent" child that contributes to miseducation in the schools, other social factors contribute to and reinforce the pervasive miseducation of young children in America today. These factors put pressure even on parents who are not caught up in the "superkid" psychology and on educators who do not subscribe to the image of the "competent" child, to engage in miseducation.

SOCIAL STATUS PRESSURES

Middle-class children of today play a different role in the family from the one they did in the past. To appreciate this new role and how it contributes to miseducation, we first have to recall the work of the gifted economist and sociologist Thorstein Veblen. In 1899 Veblen published his classic work *The Theory of the Leisure Class*. His basic argument was concisely summarized by Stuart Chase in his introduction to a later edition of the book:

> People above the line of bare subsistence in this age, and in all earlier ages, do not use the surplus which society has given them primarily for useful purposes. They do not seek to expand their lives, to live more wisely, intelligently, understandingly, but to impress other people with the fact that they have a surplus.[1]

The need to impress others with our economic surplus is as powerful in the Orient as it is in the West, and it was as strong among ancient peoples as it is today.

There are, according to Veblen, two ways in which we impress others with our economic surplus. The clearest index of economic surplus is simply not having to work. Veblen argues, for example, that the binding of noblewomen's feet in China was a symbol of leisure-class standing. A woman whose feet had been bound was in fact crippled for life and could not work: by binding her feet, parents could show that their daughter was a member of the leisure class. In Western society, high heels first became fashionable among women of the wealthy classes. They are really not utilitarian, but because they add to a woman's attractiveness, they are now worn by women of all social classes.

The second way in which we impress others with our economic surplus is by means of what Veblen called "conspicuous consumption," the expenditure of money for things whose purpose is not—or primarily not—utilitarian. Veblen makes the point that many symbols of leisure-class status do indeed have some usefulness. A Mercedes Benz, for example, certainly has utilitarian as well as status value, but the utilitarian function could easily be served by a less expensive automobile. In earlier times, the horse or carriage one drove served the same symbolic as well as utilitarian purpose. The human need, then, to impress others with our economic surplus as a sign of superior status has always been operative in American society, although its force has waxed and waned.

Indeed, after a period in the sixties and seventies when it was somewhat in disrepute, demonstrations of conspicuous consumption have, in the eighties, come back into vogue.

What has all this to do with the prevalence of miseducation in America today? Actually, a good deal, but we need to look briefly at a little socioeconomic history to see the connection. First of all, in the United States as recently as the 1950s women were the primary symbols of leisure-class status in middle-class families. Married women of a certain standing did not work because they did not have to; their husbands made enough to support them. Married women who worked were pitied or, if they had children, were regarded as at best irresponsible, given the "irrefutable" evidence of the negative effects of "maternal deprivation."

The problem with this arrangement became clear soon enough: women who did not work outside the home certainly worked very hard within it. As wives and mothers, women put in long hours (fifty hours per week, not including child care) managing a household, but they were given little credit for this and were often depicted as sitting home reading dime novels, watching television, or playing Mah-Jongg with their friends. The "I Love Lucy" television show was but one of many portrayals, during that era, of the essentially "frivolous" middle-class woman.

The women's movement in this country was motivated, in part at least, by dissatisfaction with this state of affairs. Women had become symbols of leisure-class status without the leisure, and laborers who got no credit for their labors—women who stayed at home received the benefits neither of leisure nor of labor. A consequence of the women's movement is that women are no longer symbols of a family's leisure-class standing. Today women who stay home are clearly seen as doing so out of choice—to take time off from a career, to pursue free-lance endeavors, to help infants and young children get started in life. Yet our human need to impress others with our economic excess was not diminished: new symbols of leisure-class status were required and were quickly found, in *children*.

Veblen pointed out that conspicuous consumption was often concentrated in the domains of dress, of sports, and of education. Today young children, for example, are often dressed in designer fashions bought at kiddie "boutiques." Clearly, this is more symbolic than utilitarian, for young children are hard on clothing and would be better served by outfits that were sturdy and durable rather than fashionable. Many of the sports activities of infants and young children may have some practical worth, but their significance as symbols of economic excess in most cases far outweighs their utilitarian value.

Play is no longer the thing. When the pockets of today's tots are turned out after a long day, parents are more apt to find ski-lift stubs and chunks of cello rosin than frogs, marbles and skate keys. Consider how the five-and-under set spend their day: In Atlanta at the Suzuki International Learning Center, stubby-fingered would-be virtuosos saw away on violins and cellos for tuitions that exceed $4,000 annually. At New York City's 92nd Street "Y," pint-size chefs whip up their culinary skills in a weekly one-hour class called Kids in the Kitchen for $95 a semester. On the Pacific Coast, babies barely able to hold up their heads are toning their baby fat in 45-minute workout sessions costing $5.50 at Gymboree, a Los Angeles gym for children under the age of five. And in Killington, Vt., little Jean Claude Kiddies zigzag the slopes on scaled-down skis for $15.50 a session.[2]

Putting an infant in a swimming class, or in "Gymboree," may have a little utilitarian value; but that value could easily be attained by simple activities with the parents at home. As important, or more important, is the parents' demonstration thereby, to the world at large and to their immediate social circle in particular, that they have both the money and the time to enroll their children in such classes.

The education of young children has also become a symbol of the family's economic surplus. Since the 1960s there has been a thousandfold increase in high-priced, prestigious nursery schools, some of which cater to children as young as six months of age. Although many parents consciously believe they are putting their child in the program for educational reasons, the unacknowledged reason is as likely to be a matter of status. Having a child in one of these schools is clear evidence of economic surplus:

> At the pricey Crème de la Crème preschool learning center Debra Clay's eight-month-old daughter Kendall peered at two red dots on a white flash card held by a teacher who called out, "Two." . . . Elsewhere around Crème de la Crème, 150 other tots and toddlers grappled with art, music, French and social studies until mothers and fathers in Volvos and BMW's came to pick them up.
>
> The Sidwell Friends School in Washington (tuition up to $5,000) sifts 300 applications for 28 pre-school spots so coveted that former Admissions Director Georgia Irvin received a phone call saying "We're planning to have a family and we wondered, is it really better [for admissions] to have a baby in November or April?"[3]

To be sure, parents are genuinely concerned about their children's education, but the status issue is woven in with that concern. And children themselves are very much aware of their new status as symbols of the leisure class and of conspicuous consumption. The best evidence of this new awareness is what Robert Coles describes, in his book *Privileged Ones*, as a sense of "entitlement" common among the children of affluence:

I use the word "entitlement" to describe what perhaps all quite well-off American families transmit to their children—an important psychological common denominator, I believe: an emotional expression, really, of those familiar class-bound prerogatives, money and power. . . .

Such a child, by the age of five or six, has very definite notions of what is possible, even if not always permitted; possible because there is plenty of money that can be spent. That child, in conversation and without embarrassment or the kind of reticence and secretiveness that comes later, may reveal a substantial knowledge of economic affairs.[4]

Such children are entitled to all the good things their parents provide and feel disgraced if they do not have all of the trappings they need to convey their economic surplus and their leisure-class status.

Much of the pressure contemporary parents feel with respect to dressing children in designer clothes, teaching young children academics, and giving them instruction in sports derives directly from our need to use our children to impress others with our economic surplus. We find "good" rather than real reasons for letting our children go along with the crowd; for example, if we do not go along with the crowd, we are either stingy or, what is much worse, unable to afford the symbols of leisure-class standing.

Let me illustrate the power of this kind of social status pressure with a personal example from a different era. My parents were Russian immigrants without a great deal of education. My father was a machinist and earned an adequate salary, but with six children, we were at best upper-lower-class. My mother did not work outside the home, but labored very hard within it. Although we could not afford it, one day a week we had a cleaning lady. As far as I could tell, my mother always worked harder than the cleaning lady and was never really satisfied with the work that she did, but having a cleaning lady was a social necessity for my parents; my mother could really not "hold her head up" among her friends if she did not have a cleaning lady.

The social pressure on contemporary parents to use their children as symbols of economic surplus and status is equally powerful, even if parents are not fully aware of it. The effect of being used as a symbol of conspicuous consumption seems to produce the same two reactions from children that it did from middle-class women.

One group of middle-class women rebelled and spearheaded the women's movement, which was intended—at least in part—to give women the recognition they deserved for the work they did in the home; as a result, women have attained a new independence and more freedom to choose their own life-style without social prejudice. One group of children who have been used as symbols of leisure-class status reacts in much the same way. Their rebellion, however, does not often occur until adolescence, when young people reconstruct their childhood to discover that they have been exploited and used. How such youngsters rebel will depend in part upon the dominant orientation of their parents. For example, the child of Gourmet parents may "go native" (which currently is the "punk" style) and reject all the graces the parents have tried to instill. The child of a College-Degree couple may drop out of school or perform poorly; a child too long in sports may burn out in adolescence and refuse to participate; pressured Prodigy children may often show symptoms of emotional disturbance in adolescence.

To be sure, this does not always happen, because each family is different and the extent to which status concerns predominate over other motives will determine how any particular child reacts. And the period of rebellion may have a healthy aftermath if it leads, as it did with the women's movement, to a new sense of independence and freedom on the part of young people to choose their own individual life course.

On the other hand, some youngsters may rebel so strongly that they will lose valuable years trying to find themselves.

The second reaction to being used as a symbol of leisure-class status is to accept that status as one's due. It has to be admitted that at least some middle-class women came to believe that they were entitled to leisure-class status and resented any suggestion that they should have to work, inside the home or outside. They had been reared to think that marrying was the ultimate goal in life, and they now enjoyed their status as symbols of economic surplus.

The women's movement was particularly hard upon this group of women: going out into the world and pursuing a career was the last thing they wanted to do, but they could no longer simply stay home, either. Such women often went off on voyages of discovery, taking courses, trying out various jobs, and often destroying their marriages into the bargain. They became deeply resentful of their husbands' careers and of other women who were successfully pursuing theirs. They wanted the fruits of a career, but did not really know how to put in the time and effort required. Often they rationalized that men or women who were successful "enjoyed" their work, which came "easy" to them, and often they became bitter, seemingly angry at the world but really angry at themselves.

As children become symbols of leisure-class status, a significant portion of these young people will also fall prey to the "to the manor born" outlook. In their minds such things as a car or trips abroad, which previous generations assumed they must work for and pay for themselves, become simply their due. These youths—and the number will increase as more and more infants and young children are used as symbols of leisure status—will assume that they are naturally entitled to, say, a college education and that it is not something they have to work for or contribute to.

The danger here is that such young people may not "find" themselves even after they complete their education. They may expect to make a quick killing in the stock market, or become rich by writing a hit song or by inheritance from a rich relative. Although they may work and pursue a career, they are not really fully committed because of their feeling deep down that they are entitled *a priori* and by nature to leisure-class status. If we treat infants and young children as if they were members of the privileged class, can we really expect them to feel otherwise after they grow up?

Many older wealthy families have learned to instill a sense of public service in their offspring. But newly affluent middle-class parents have not acquired this skill. We are using our children as symbols of leisure-class standing without building in safeguards against an overweening sense of entitlement—a sense of entitlement that may incline some young people more toward the good life than toward the hard work that, for most of us, makes the good life possible.

COMPETITIVE PARENTING PRESSURES

We are a competitive society. We compete at work and at play, with our relatives and friends as well as with our enemies. But parents today have become more competitive than ever before. In large measure this reflects the increased competitiveness of the workplace nationally and internationally.

When the United States was unquestionably superior to other countries in productivity and technological progress, we could be beneficent to other countries. After the Second World War we rehabilitated devastated Europe with the Marshall Plan, and we imposed democracy upon Japan and underwrote the rebuilding of its industrial base. In the last two decades, however, our steel industry, our automobile industry, our shoe industry, our textile plants, our farm production are all being challenged from abroad. We import most of our watches, television sets, radios, and cameras. Our computer industry is in constant competition with Japan.

These new challenges from outside our country have eroded our economic security and exacerbated an already overheated national competitiveness. The transformation of our society from an industrial to a postindustrial information and service economy, which now employs more than 70 percent of the population, has radically changed the work environment and job opportunities.[5] Technology is constantly rendering some professions and skills obsolete: dictation equipment, which seemed a godsend only a decade ago, is quickly being rendered obsolete by word processors; a taxi driver told me that his uniform rental and cleaning service was put out of business when new fabrics were devised that the wearers could take home and wash themselves.

Parents see that getting ahead in today's society will be difficult and that the competition for getting into the professions and high-paying managerial and other positions will be tighter than ever before. They want to give their child every possible chance to "make it." Competitive parents believe that they can give their children the best chance at making it if they make their children highly competitive as well. Judith Martin, in her book *Miss Manners' Guide to Raising Perfect Children*, comments that "your truly competitive parent loses no opportunity to enter his child into competition, beginning with its birthweight."[6]

This sense of competitiveness is a common denominator of all of the "superkid" parenting styles described in Chapter 2, but in some parents having a competitive child seems to be an end in itself:

When Linda Hale cuddles baby Kevin, she sometimes wears a bow-tied dress-for-success blouse. That's perhaps appropriate, since the former executive secretary regards modern motherhood as an intensely serious business. Kevin's brother, Bryan, three, barely managed to squeeze into the last opening in their Boston suburb's Montessori school, and his engineer father, Bruce Hale, is coaching him in reading and arithmetic with nightly storybook and flashcard sessions. The Hales hope that nine-week-old Kevin will eventually toddle in his sibling's footsteps. Even though tuition is nearly $2,000 a year per child, they're convinced it's a no-choice investment. "There's so much pressure to get into college," says 38-year-old Linda. "You have to start them young and push them toward their goal [*sic*]. They have to be aware of everything—the alphabet, numbers, reading. I want to fill these little sponges as much as possible."[7]

Soon after 15-month-old John Sampar finishes breakfast at his family's Fairfax Station kitchen, the lessons begin.

Some days, his father Bill starts with Russian flash cards on the living-room sofa. Other days it might be algebra. This summer John especially likes identifying birds.

"He's just amazing," boasts Bill Sampar, 53, who says he quit his $30,000-a-year job as an electrical engineer to teach his son. Sampar's first child, John, he says, can now recognize 700 words and identify all 30 books on the boy's shelf. "The other day I asked him what seven times seven plus one equaled and showed him two different cards. He picked the one with 50. He had never done that before.

"I have no set plans about what I would like him to be," says Sampar of the results of his daily routine, "I just want him to have all of his options."[8]

Although the "earlier is better" psychology of the "superkid" and the image of the "competent" child are the major forces in pushing parental competitiveness down to the early-childhood level, there is another factor as well. This was the choice of the term "Head Start" for programs designed to give disadvantaged young children the educational experience and health care that might move them up to the academic norm. The choice was an unfortunate one, inasmuch as "Head Start" suggests that education is a race and that children in the program have an advantage in that race. Almost inevitably, this aroused or intensified a concern among middle-class parents that their own small children receive a "head start" as well.

The Head Start idea thus helped trigger a latent parental competitiveness which in the past did not appear until children were much older, but which is nowadays already evident with respect to infants and young children. This competitiveness is encouraged, perhaps unwittingly, by professionals, by the media, and by the availability of high-pressure programs of early education. Middle-class parents are as much victims as they are perpetrators of the situation. But the consequence— the conception of education as a race—is something to be concerned about: education has always been competitive, but when it is viewed as a race, the competitive dimension looms far out of proportion to other aspects of education, including active engagement in learning.

Education is not a race. A child who learns to read at age three has in no way "won" over a child who learns to read at age six or seven. A true race has a well-marked finish line that all participants must cross to determine the winner. In contrast, "learning to read" is a lifelong process. For example, I did not really learn how to read Freud until I was a postdoctoral fellow, when my teacher, David Rapaport, painstakingly guided me through one of Freud's books page by page. The same is true for every facet of education, whether it be science, math, or literature: there are no finish lines. Learning does not stop after we have learned a skill or left school or college; learning and education are lifelong processes that come to an end only when we do.

If education is not a race, neither is competitiveness a necessary characteristic of academic achievement. In a review of 122 studies conducted between 1924 and 1981 which compared achievement in cooperative as opposed to competitive classrooms, the results were impressively in favor of cooperation. The authors concluded that: "a) cooperation is considerably more effective than interpersonal competition and individualist efforts, b) cooperation with intergroup competition is also superior to interpersonal competition and individualistic efforts."[9]

Similar results were found for the effects of individual competitiveness. In a study that related scientific visibility to competitiveness, highly visible scientists scored high on measures of work involvement and sense of mastery but low on measures of competitiveness.[10] And the results hold for business people as well. When success in business was measured by salary, investigators found that the most successful business people (the most highly paid) also scored lower on competitiveness than did the less successful business people.[11] These results are not really surprising; they are exactly what those who have studied successful businesses report as well.[12]

Instilling a sense that education is a race and that competitiveness is essential to achievement miseducates children. Rather than preparing them for success, it may put them at risk of failure, or at least of doing more poorly than they might otherwise do.

COMPUTER PRESSURE

The introduction of personal computers has, in many ways, provided still another domain for the use of children as symbols of leisure-class status and for parental competitiveness. In addition, it has confounded the ideas about the importance of early-childhood education with the assumption that computer "literacy" at an early age is the royal road to a successful career in postindustrial society. We need to look at each of these facets of computer pressure on the education of young children.

Computers as Symbols of Leisure-Class Status

Personal computers, particularly the more advanced ones, are expensive. One can easily spend as much for a home computer, printer, software, and service contracts as for the family car. On the other hand, for most families, home computers have little if any practical utility. To be sure, computers can facilitate the work of professionals such as writers, accountants, and stockbrokers, but they really are not a great advantage in balancing checkbooks, preparing one's income tax return, or paying the monthly bills. For family life, as opposed to business or professional life, personal computers have yet to prove themselves, and their purchase cannot be justified on purely utilitarian grounds.

It is true, of course, that many of us purchase a home computer because we have heard it will be beneficial to our children's education. Most children, however, have access to computers at school, where they are used mainly as word processors, as calculators, and for information retrieval. Having a computer at home is a convenience, but is in no way essential for a child to acquire computer literacy.

Many of us are nonetheless buying elaborate computer systems with expensive software programs. Such purchases may reasonably be regarded, in part at least, as exercises in conspicuous consumption. Children who can talk about their hard-disc systems and their laser printers might as well be talking about their Ralph Lauren shirts and Bally shoes. For many families, computers have become yet another symbol of leisure-class status.

For the children, the blessing is a mixed one. For some children the home computer may reveal a hitherto unexpected talent and aptitude, and so the possession of a computer of one's own makes that child a member of a very special elite with its own language and rituals, what Sherry Terkle[13] calls, in *The Second Self*, a "computer culture." While participation in such a culture can be positive for self-esteem, it can also be ego-inflating and can contribute to condescending attitudes toward others who are not conversant with computers. For such youngsters, being a "computernik" can be socially isolating. Like other symbols of leisure-class status, computer competence can lead to social rejection by those less fortunate.

Many children do find computers fascinating. I now use the computer in my office as an adjunct to play therapy. The ways in which children interact with the computer reflect the ways in which they interact with the world. Generally, socially outgoing children are less interested in the computer than are children who are more introverted and socially isolated. Such children live a great deal "in their heads" and find computers a way of extending and enhancing this inner life. The computer productions of such children are as revealing as their Rorschach responses.

The imposition of a personal style upon a home computer is not always beneficial. Some children use the computer to further isolate and distance themselves from other people.

> Henry is such a child. He was having a difficult time before he met computers and learned to program. The computer did not create a problem where none existed, but he is an example of a kind of child for whom the computer may reinforce patterns of isolation and help lock [him] into a world of getting lost in things at the expense of the development of relationships with other people.[14]

When computers are purchased as symbols of economic surplus, they can contribute to the child's sense of entitlement and to the consequences of that syndrome. The computer can have other consequences, both positive and negative, depending upon the child's personality.

Computers and Parental Competition

Computer literacy, like early reading and many other skills, has become another weapon in the arsenal of parental competition. We now brag about our child's accomplishments on the computer with the same pride and satisfaction that parents of earlier generations boasted about their child's playing the violin. And there is really no harm and some benefit for a child whose parents are pleased and proud of his or her accomplishments.

The real problem with the entrance of computers into the arena of parental competitiveness occurs when it becomes enmeshed in the "superkid" and the "earlier is better" psychology. Many parents want to start their preschool children on computers as yet another way in which to give them an "edge" over the competition. A number of companies have produced "math" and "reading" programs for young children, and programs such as LOGO seek to teach young children programming.

The introduction of computers into early education, in part to satisfy parental concerns, is a good example of miseducation. In the first place, computers are complex machines not easily understood by young children; to be accessible to them, the computers must be transformed into expensive teaching machines. The earlier teaching machines did not work: the reason is not, as is often reported, because there were not enough good programs or software; the problem with teaching machines is the theory of learning that generates the programs.

Programmed instruction, whether presented on a computer or on a teaching machine, provides information in a graded sequence of steps with alternate routes if errors are made along the way. The theory of learning upon which such programs was based was developed primarily from animal research. Contemporary learning theorists recognize that learning principles are not the same across all animal species, and that in many ways they are species-specific. Even young children learn in ways that are infinitely more complex than the modes of learning employed by the highest animals. Programmed instruction doesn't work with children for a very simple reason: it is boring!

Programmed learning is boring because it ignores an all-important principle of learning that the Swiss psychologist Jean Piaget called "assimilation." Traditional learning theorists, such as B. F. Skinner, upon whose theories of learning much programmed instruction is based, define learning as "the modification of behavior as a result of experience." But Piaget, while recognizing this as one mode of learning, points out that children also "assimilate" or transform experience to conform to their individual existing modes of thought. From this standpoint, learning is also "the modification of experience as a result of behavior." Children are not just passive absorbers of information; rather, they constantly transform information to fit with their existing modes of thought.

The following dialogue about computers gives evidence of the kind of transformation of information that children always enjoy and engage in whenever they are given the chance:

Robert (age 7) throws Merlin [a computer toy that plays ticktacktoe] into the sand in anger and frustration. "Cheater, I hope your brains break." He is overheard by Craig and Greg, aged six and eight, who sense that this may be a good time to reclaim Merlin for themselves. They salvage the by now very sandy toy and take it upon themselves to set Robert straight.

Craig: "Merlin doesn't know if it cheats. It won't know

if it breaks. It doesn't know if you break it. Robert, it's not alive."

Greg: "Someone taught Merlin to play. But he doesn't know if he wins or loses."

Robert: "Yes, he does know if he loses. He makes different noises."[15]

Each child interprets the experience of Merlin in a different way, depending upon his level of mental ability and past experience. Programmed learning ignores what children bring to the learning situation and their need and capacity to transform what they encounter into something in keeping with their present view of the world. It is because programmed instruction provides no opportunity for children's creative interaction that they find it so dull and uninteresting.

Putting computers into early-childhood programs as teaching machines may thus produce an effect opposite to the one intended: early programmed instruction that children find boring and frustrating may encourage a strong dislike for computers. Computers as teaching machines in early-childhood education are thus a good example of miseducation; it puts children at risk for negative attitudes and failure without reasonable justification.

Computers and Mental Development

The introduction of home computers has been so rapid that no one knows what their impact upon the mental development and academic achievement of children will really be. There are at least three schools of opinion on this matter. One sees the computer as a powerful new tool for enhancing human intellectual potential. Proponents believe that all children should learn programming because they will not only be prepared to use computers, but will also develop their reasoning and problem-solving skills. Seymour Papert, a major exponent of this point of view, has introduced a simplified computer language, LOGO, for use by children.

A second school argues that the computer is no different from any other technological innovation. Such innovations extend our capacities without altering them. Telescopes and microscopes, for example, enable us to observe things at a greater distance or in more detail than is possible with the naked eye, but our visual capacities are not really changed by looking through a telescope or microscope. From this point of view, the computer extends our intelligence, particularly our memory abilities, without changing those abilities in the process. Accordingly, learning to operate a computer is useful for exactly the same reason that learning to type and to operate a calculator is useful, to enable us to work more efficiently and rapidly.

Still a third school of thought argues that while computers are a new technology that extends our capacities, there is no need to learn any special computer skills to utilize this technology. Eventually, this group of writers hold, computer technology will be made so accessible that no special computer skills will need to be learned in order to access the extensions of capacity the computer has to offer. For example, we can use automated tellers in banks without any special computer skills, even though the whole transaction is run by computers.

In fact, there is likely to be a little truth in each of these positions. As I will describe below, there is a way in which computers can contribute to mental development; we just aren't there yet in terms of technology. Likewise, the use of computers for such activities as writing and information retrieval will probably always require the acquisition of certain access skills such as typing and knowledge of word-processing programs. And finally, it is also true that in many other domains we may be able to access computers without the acquisition of any special skills.

We need to consider now the way in which computers might contribute to mental development. If computers are developed to the point where even young children can interact with them simply and directly, mental development might be enhanced. Jean Piaget's theory of intelligence—adaptive thought and action—describes a process of "reflective abstraction" whereby children abstract from their actions upon objects in the real world. What children abstract, however, is not some image of the materials acted upon, but, rather, a mental representation of the actions that they had performed on the things. These abstracted actions become internalized mental abilities that allow us to do in our heads what once we had to do with our hands.

Piaget was, of course, talking about children operating directly upon materials in the environment. He gave the example of a child arranging and rearranging ten little stones on the ground. The child arranged them first in a square, then in a circle, and then in a diamond. At one point the child simply said, "They are still ten." His discovery did not come from a passive observation of the different forms but, rather, from his active construction of them. What the child abstracted was not some visual template but rather the reversible actions that changed the appearance of the stones without changing the number.

Geometric forms are also learned by reflective abstraction. A child who manipulates a set of wooden forms begins to abstract their different motor paths. A circle is an unending path, a triangle has three turns, and so on. Once the motor actions are internalized, the child can recognize any circle, triangle, or square no matter what its size or what it is made of. What the child has learned is not some "ideal image" of a circle, triangle, or square but an internalized set of actions that allows the child to identify new exemplars of the forms.

Working with a computer is far different from these examples. In fact, the computer is still sufficiently complex that to operate it well enough to interact with one's own mind, one must already have a fairly high level of mental development. It is for this reason that I do not believe that programs such as LOGO promote mental development. The problem with such programs is that they presuppose a level of mental ability higher than that which they seek to encourage. Put differently, a child who really understands programming is at a sufficiently high level of mental development that learning programming is not really going to promote additional mental development.

Does this mean that, for the present, computers have no role in mental growth? Not at all. I think that grade school children who learn to use simple word-processing programs are confronted with their own thought processes and that this can be beneficial for mental development. The computer, then, can provide another avenue for children to engage in the "reflective abstraction" that encourages the formation of new mental abilities. With succeeding generations of computer languages, even young children may be able to interact with computers in ways that would permit reflective abstraction. But we are not there yet, and, for the present, computers that present programmed learning to young children are examples of miseducation.

THE RISKS OF
MISEDUCATION

5

Trust and Autonomy Versus Mistrust, Shame, and Doubt

HUMAN DEVELOPMENT CAN be seen, according to Erik Erikson in *Childhood and Society*, as a series of psychosocial "crises"—critical periods for the realization of opposed personality potentials. At birth, these potentials exist as paired opposites, and during the "crisis" period a person's experience determines which of the two opposed personality potentials will be the stronger. Erikson's model of personality development also describes the kinds of experience that determine which personality potential will outweigh the other.

Four of Erikson's crises occur in the early-childhood period, and in my work I have encountered an additional two pairs of personality potentials that also have their crises during the early years of life. Inasmuch as the resolution of these crises is very much determined by the kind of parenting and schooling a child receives, Erikson's model provides a useful framework for looking at the risks of miseducation.

TRUST VERSUS MISTRUST

During the first year of life, Erikson says, the infant's task is to acquire a sense of *trust* that is stronger than his or her sense of *mistrust*. The sense of trust involves a feeling that the world is a safe place and that one's needs will be met. The sense of mistrust, on the other hand, involves the sense that the world is unsafe and unreliable, not trustworthy. Erikson points out that a certain degree of mistrust is healthy for a child. A child who is too trusting and altogether lacking in caution—who is, for example, willing to accompany anyone who asks him to —may encounter difficulties. The important thing for each pair of personality potentials is that the positive one be stronger than the negative one.

The sense of trust is to a large extent a derivative of the child's attachment or "bonding" to the parents. The initial stage of attachment takes place during the first three months of life. During the first stage the infant engages in a number of general social actions that capture parental attention. Such actions include looking at the parent's face, cuddling when held in the parent's arms, and smiling, cooing, and crying. All of these actions tend to elicit general reactions of concern, caring, and amusement on the part of the parents, which attach the parents to the child. In the same way, the parent's positive reactions to the baby's actions attach the infant to the parents as well as encouraging the infant's sense of trust in them.

At the next stage the baby becomes much more specific and selective in his or her social communications. The baby will smile and coo at the parent, but not at a stranger. The infant will snuggle when held by the parent, but may stiffen and cry when held by a stranger. Now the baby can make the distinction between parent and non-parent even at a distance. The baby's preference for the parent is a powerful reinforcer for the parent's attachment to the infant. There is nothing like a baby who coos up at you, and ignores or shies away from another person, to bolster one's ego. There is something special about being special to somebody else, particularly a baby.

At the next stage, which can start as early as six months

but usually appears during the last trimester of the first year —after the child has constructed the notion of the parent as a permanent object (an object that exists for the child even when it is not present to the child's senses)—the baby actively seeks to be near to and have contact with the parent. Earlier, when the baby cried, it was in part to get the mother's attention, in part to get relief from hunger, thirst, or discomfort. But now the child cries, gurgles, coos, and begins to say words with the prime purpose of making contact with the parent. These initiatives are furthered by the child's enhanced mobility. The child will crawl toward the parent, will hold up its arms to indicate a wish to be picked up and held, and will show dismay at the parent's departure. It is at this stage that one can say with some assurance whether or not the infant is truly attached and has a healthy sense of trust.

In the infant, this attachment is experienced as a sense of security in the presence of the parent and a sense of trust that the parent will meet the child's needs. In parents, the sense of attachment is experienced as a feeling of love, caring, and protectiveness. Research[1] suggests that children who are securely attached to their parents at twelve to eighteen months were later rated (by their preschool teachers) as more emotionally positive, more empathetic, and more compliant than children who were less securely attached. In effect, they were more "trusting" than were children with less solid attachments.

Does the foregoing discussion mean that leaving an infant in a day-care center or with an in-house baby-sitter during the day puts the child's attachment to parents and sense of trust in jeopardy? No! First of all, it appears that the infant's attachment to and trust in the parent is not, or at least not primarily, dependent upon the parent's meeting the baby's biological needs. A baby does not automatically become attached to the person who feeds and changes him or her, and so on. Likewise, it does not appear that bonding is determined by the absolute amount of time the baby is with particular adults. A baby, for example, can be with adults other than the mother for more time than with the mother and still be primarily attached to the mother.[2]

What does seem critical for the establishment of attachment and trust is the parent's attitude and receptivity to the child's communications. Perhaps because we are genuinely committed to the infant, and to a long-term relationship, we interact differently with our baby than does a care-giver. We are more sensitive to the variety of different messages babies send through their body language and their gurgles and cries. Again, the success of this interaction is not solely dependent upon us as parents. Equally, it depends upon the effectiveness with which the infant communicates to us. Effective attachment and a solid sense of trust depend upon this wonderfully elaborate nonverbal discourse we have with our baby.

In contrast, a care-giver does not feel and cannot convey commitment to a long-term relationship with the infant. Care-givers are wary of becoming attached to the infant because they know that at one point or another the attachment will be broken and they do not want to subject themselves to the pain of that loss.

Child care-givers become attached to a certain degree, of course—otherwise they would not be human—but they also develop strategies for distancing themselves from becoming too involved. I recall working for a short time in the cancer ward of a children's hospital. The nurses somehow learned to be loving and caring toward their patients without at the same time becoming too attached. They knew that many of the children would not leave the ward alive. Although this is an extreme case, it highlights the reason why care-givers of infants and young children do not manifest the attitudes that would encourage strong bonding on the part of the infant.

Not surprisingly, then, the research strongly suggests that infants are attached to and trust their parents, even when they have been cared for since the early months of life by a care-giver for a considerable portion of the day.* Does this mean that "quality time" is really the critical factor? Certainly the quality of the interaction between parent and child is critical to the attachment. Something of the parent's long-term commitment, caring, and concern comes through to the infant even in brief interactions. But a certain quantity of time is necessary to convey commitment and to encourage trust. Quality time is really not enough; quantity is essential, too. But it is reassuring to know that the quantity of time we commit to routine care-giving is sufficient to secure attachment and trust.

What, then, constitutes miseducation in the first year of life? To answer this question, it is helpful to distinguish between "warm" and "cold" interactions with an infant. Warm interactions encourage attachment and a sense of trust; cold interactions mar attachment and encourage distrust. By and large, we spontaneously engage in "warm" inter-actions because of love for, and enjoyment in, our infant. Such interactions are spontaneous and effortless. In contrast, many cold interactions are deliberate and are experienced as effortful.

We engage in warm interactions when, during the course of routine caring activities, such as feeding, changing, bathing, and comforting the baby, we accompany our ministrations with talk, cuddling, singing, and playing. We tell the baby in many different ways that we like him or her as a person and really enjoy his or her company. By showing our attachment in a warm, lively way, we encourage attachment and trust on the part of our baby.

In contrast, cold interactions are task- rather than child-

*This conclusion holds only when the non-parental care is of high quality.

oriented. They involve demands, stern looks and words, and the threat of punishment or, what is worse, the threat of withdrawal of love. Of course, some cold interactions are inevitable, particularly when the baby does something potentially dangerous and our harsh words and tones come from our anxiety about the baby's welfare. But even young infants seem to know the difference between cold interactions that are for their benefit and those that are not.

We may put the child's attachment and sense of trust at risk by imposing adult learning priorities that of necessity are task- rather than child-oriented. I recall observing a mother showing flash cards to her six-month-old. The baby was squirming and looking every which way but at the cards. But the mother insisted, and eventually the baby threw up on its bib (expressing my sentiments exactly). Yet the mother was too caught up in the teaching and proclaimed, "If you stick with it, they will come through for you." Perhaps, but at the risk of impairing a healthy sense of trust and promoting a strong sense of distrust.

An abiding sense of attachment and a healthy sense of trust are fundamental to later healthy interpersonal relationships. A child who has learned to attach to and trust a parent has the basis for later attaching to and trusting friends and eventually a mate. But attachment and trust are also critical to learning. Freud recognized this fact when he argued that the "transference" (the patient's attachment to and trust in the therapist) is critical to the patient's readiness to change (learn) and profit from therapy. In the same way, many children learn to read in part because they are attached to and trust parents who are readers and who reward the child's progress in reading. As Dr. Spock says:

> Before they begin formal schooling, children can be strongly
> motivated to learn to read if they have parents who read
> to them. As they become intellectually capable of discrim-

inating letter shapes, they may ask the names and sounds of letters. They will want to go to school unless alienated by bad experiences.[3]

Engaging in unnecessary cold interactions with infants in order to teach them some tricks such as recognizing words, pictures, or numbers from flash cards is miseducation. The child is put at risk for an impaired attachment and sense of mistrust. And because attachment is critical to later learning, the parent who engages an infant in cold interactions with the aim of giving the child an edge in academics may be doing just the opposite. The child may be handicapped because the attachment and trust essential for effective later learning have been impaired. And since there is absolutely no evidence that instructing infants has any lasting benefits, the infant is put at risk for absolutely no purpose.

A couple of other characteristics of attachment and trust need to be described. It is important to point out here that healthy attachment and trust can appear in many different and disguised ways. Devoted parents who give their children much warm interaction are sometimes upset when it appears that the infant prefers some other adult to themselves. But this is only an appearance. I recall an event that occurred at a day-care center where I was doing some work. At the end of the day, about five-thirty, a father came to pick up his ten-month-old daughter, who had been in the center all day. The father was a single parent rearing three children, two of whom were in public school and whom he would pick up from their after-school baby-sitter once he had collected his little girl.

When he came into the room, his daughter, who was in the arms of a day-care worker, began to sob and cling to the worker's shoulder. I saw the father's face, and the pain and hurt made me almost turn away. I knew this particular father, knew that his wife had taken off only months before with another man. I knew that when he got home, he prepared the evening meal, bathed the children and got them to bed, and spent the rest of the evening washing up, doing the laundry, and getting things ready for the next day. His reward was seeing his children well cared for and happy, as well as enjoying their affection for him.

I knew that when he saw his daughter apparently preferring the day-care worker to him, he felt terribly rejected. Fortunately, I had been around the center all day and was able to reassure the father that his daughter's behavior was really not what it appeared to be. The day at the nursery school had been chaotic, with one crisis after the other. Through all of this, his daughter had quietly played in her crib. It was only when she saw her father, felt the security of his presence, that she allowed herself to cry.

Another feature of the infant's attachment to and trust in parents can have a less happy outcome. Some parents who succeed in giving their child a healthy sense of attachment and trust during the first year of life may nonetheless abuse this attachment and trust at later ages. Once a child attaches to and trusts a parent, the enormous motivating force of attachment and trust can be used to engage children in miseducation. A young child, for example, may seem to be enjoying ballet, or tennis, or violin lessons when in fact what the child is really doing is attempting to please parents to whom he or she is attached.

Many parents who have enrolled their young child in ballet, tennis, or violin find this point rather hard to accept. Again and again, when talking to these parents, I have been told, "But she loves the ballet lessons and would be devastated if I stopped them." It is certainly true that some young children may genuinely come to enjoy the lessons, particularly if they have a sensitive, thoughtful teacher attuned to their prodigious but nevertheless limited repertoire of abilities. But for the majority of children taking such lessons, the major motivation is to please their parents. It was, after all, the parents, not the child, who decided on the lessons in the first place. What does a three- or four-year-old know of ballet, tennis, or violin?

Sometimes the miseducation of children by means of attachment is unconscious but nonetheless lethal. A syndrome that I have dealt with in older children illustrates how the attachment of a child to a parent can be abused. I first encountered this syndrome when I was running a school for what we called "curriculum-disabled" children (children of average ability who were functioning below the academic norm for their age). During our second year we enrolled a child who was a real puzzle to us all. Since that time I have seen a number of youngsters like her, and for lack of a better term I call them "impossible" children.

A description of this particular young girl will illustrate the syndrome. She was eight years old, thin, and average-looking and had a high-pitched, whiny voice. She first came to my attention when the weather turned cold (the school was in Rochester, New York). She came to school in a thin coat and a halter and skirt that were more appropriate for summer. In addition, the lunches she brought were something of a scandal. They included, as often as not, such items as empty ice cream cones and uncooked pasta. Sympathetic teachers and other children often shared their lunches with her.

Yet at school she was a thoroughly obnoxious child. She destroyed other children's work, threw tantrums if she did not get her way, and stole things from other children and from the school. At first we tried to use the universal panacea, tender loving care—TLC, still convinced, in our naïveté, that love would solve all problems. It worked for a time: she seemed more pleasant and tractable. But then, just as we let our guard down, she would strike again.

I called the parents in for a conference to see whether we

might take some concerted action. Slowly, as the mother and father talked, a new picture emerged that I had not seen before. The couple did not have a good relationship, and the mother did not appear to be attached either to the child or to the father. Further, it became clear that this mother wanted, and in effect needed, an impossible child.

Although she was not attached to the child, she was sufficiently aware of social opinion to know that she could not openly reject her daughter. And so, in many subliminal ways, such as by letting the child make her own lunch and choose what clothes she would wear, the mother encouraged her to be an impossible child. For if her daughter was impossible, as we had all acknowledged, then her rejection of such a child was both understandable and acceptable. By using her daughter's attachment to her to get the child to behave in impossible ways, the mother was able publicly to reject her without embarrassment or social disapproval.

Granted, such children are the exception rather than the rule, but they indicate the power of the attachment and trust between parents and children. We miseducate children when we put that attachment and trust at risk by unnecessary cold interactions during the first year of life, or by misuse of that attachment and trust at later ages. On the other hand, a child who has experienced predominantly warm interactions will attain a strong sense of attachment and healthy sense of trust that will form the foundation for strong interpersonal relations and effective learning as he or she matures.

AUTONOMY VERSUS SHAME AND DOUBT

During the second and third years of life, children gain increasing control over their bodies. Toddlers have begun to walk, to climb, to hold and to drop, to feed themselves, and may even indicate a readiness for toilet training. Erikson says the emergence of these motor abilities sets the stage for the next personality crisis, namely, that of *autonomy* versus *shame* and *doubt*. If the parent encourages the child to attain various motor skills for which the child appears ready, the child will attain a strong sense of autonomy, of being in control of himself or herself. In later life, the sense of autonomy appears as a healthy sense of independence, a willingness to take a stand and to take responsibility for one's beliefs and actions.

On the other hand, if the parent imposes motor training too early and/or ridicules, laughs at, or gets angry at the child's failures, the child will experience a sense of shame at the public failure and a sense of doubt as to his or her ability to control his or her body. If parents persist in this course, the child's sense of shame and doubt may exceed the sense of autonomy. Erikson describes the consequences this way:

> If denied the gradual and well-guided experience of the autonomy of free choice (or if, indeed, weakened by an initial loss of trust) the child will turn against himself all of his urge to discriminate and to manipulate. He will overmanipulate himself, he will develop a precocious conscience. Instead of taking possession of things in order to test them by purposeful repetition, he will become obsessed by his own repetitiveness. By such obsessiveness, of course, he then learns to repossess the environment and to regain power by stubborn and minute control, where he could not find large-scale mutual regulation. Such hollow victory is the infantile model for a compulsion neurosis. It is also the infantile source of later attempts in adult life to govern by the letter, rather than by the spirit.[4]

And with respect to shame: Shame is an emotion insufficiently studied, because in our civilization it is so early and easily absorbed by guilt. Shame supposes that one is completely exposed and conscious of being looked at: in one word, self-conscious. One is visible and not ready to be visible; which is why we dream of shame as a situation in which we are stared at in a condition of complete undress, in night attire, "with one's pants down." Shame is early expressed in an impulse to bury one's face, or to sink, right then and there, into the ground. But this, I think, is essentially rage turned against the self. He who is ashamed would like to force the world not to look at him, not to notice his exposure. . . . Too much shaming does not lead to genuine propriety but to a secret determination to try and get away with things, unseen, if indeed, it does not result in a defiant shamelessness.[5]

In his writing, Erikson has built upon and extended Freud's ideas regarding infantile sexuality and later character formation. While Erikson extends his theory to motor training in general, Freud limited his interpretations to tracing the relationships between specific types of motor training in childhood and character traits in adulthood.

The persons whom I am about to describe are remarkable for a regular combination of the three following peculiarities: they are exceptionally orderly, parsimonious and obstinate. Each of these words covers a small group or series of traits which are related to one another. Orderly comprises both bodily cleanliness and reliability and conscientiousness in the performance of petty duties: the opposite would be untidy or negligent. Parsimony may be exaggerated up to the point of avarice; and obstinacy may amount to defiance with which irascibility and vindictiveness may well be associated. The two latter qualities—parsimony and obstinacy—hang together more closely than the third, orderliness; they are, too, the more constant element in the whole complex. It seems to me, however, incontestable that all three may in some way belong together.[6]

Freud explained his observations by reference to his theory of infantile sexuality.* During the early years of life, first the oral and then the anal zones of the body are the focuses of sexual pleasure. Children who get extraordinary pleasure from the anal zone retain for longer than necessary, for the pleasure of it, and as a result become fixated on "keeping" and "not letting go" as pleasurable modes of activity. In adulthood, this translates into the "keeping and not letting go" of money (parsimony) and "keeping and not letting go" of ideas (obstinacy), as well as the "keeping and not letting go" of things (orderliness).

Thus, for both Erikson and Freud, from somewhat different theoretical perspectives, motor training has important consequences for later personality formation. Given this importance, it is instructive to review first what is generally regarded as healthy toilet training before reviewing some other motor skill areas that can be critical for determining whether the child's sense of autonomy will outweigh his or her sense of shame and guilt.

Toilet Training

Because no two children are exactly alike and children follow their own individual developmental timetables, there is no hard and fast rule for when to begin toilet training. Such

---

*It is important to recall that Freud, in speaking of infantile sexuality, employed the term "sexuality" in the broad sense as a pattern of gradual arousal and sudden diminution of excitation that is common to the drives of eating, elimination, and sexual gratification. Hunger, for example, builds slowly after several hours but is diminished quickly when we ingest food. Likewise, the need for elimination builds slowly and is quickly reduced when elimination occurs. The sexual drive obviously has the same pattern. It is in this broad sense, then, of their sharing the same pattern of gradual buildup and sudden diminution of excitation that the infant's eating and elimination can be described as "sexual."

training can be accomplished only after the child has acquired a certain degree of muscular control and after the nervous system is sufficiently well developed. The ability of a child to become aware of bowel or bladder fullness, and then to exercise muscular control over those organs, clearly involves a complex coordination of intellectual, emotional, and motor skills that is dependent, in part at least, upon the maturity of the nervous system.

In general, bowel training precedes bladder training, and such training is usually easier and more successful when undertaken between 18 and 28 months. About 80 percent of children are toilet-trained by 27.7 months. As their nervous systems mature, toddlers get signals when their bowel or bladder is full, and they discover that they can help the process of evacuation by contracting or relaxing their muscles. They also discover that they can "hold back" and delay the evacuation. As toddlers acquire the rudiments of language, they begin to associate certain words with the feelings and exertions they are experiencing.

When we believe a child is ready for toilet training, having seen that the child is becoming aware of his or her movements, we can put the child on a potty chair at about the time the toddler usually has a bowel movement, often after breakfast. We need to tell the child what we want him or her to do. We can do this by saying something like "Let go." While it is important to praise the child for success, it is also important not to get upset if the child does not succeed at once, or has occasional setbacks.

A caution: it is not a good idea to initiate toilet training at times of emotional upheaval in the family, such as the birth of a new sibling, a move to a new house, or a visit from grandparents. Effective toilet training requires a comfortable, relaxed atmosphere for both parent and child. If there is tension and turmoil in the household at the time you feel toilet training should begin, it is much better to postpone this training until the situation quiets down. Nothing is lost, and there is much to be gained by holding off toilet training for a month or two so that you can begin when the atmosphere is more calm and relaxed.

I HAVE GONE into detail about toilet training because it is the first activity where the parent really needs to intervene and teach the toddler. Although it might appear simple, we have seen how complex toilet training really is. Toilet training must wait upon the child's physical maturation as well as upon intellectual and emotional development. The introduction of appropriate toilet training requires careful observation on the part of the parent, not to mention a great deal of patience and good humor. By its complexity, by how it must be individualized, and by its demands upon parent and child, appropriate toilet training is a good example of healthy education and a standard against which to measure motor miseducation.

It has to be emphasized that regardless of the motor ability we are encouraging, a healthy sense of autonomy must be balanced with a certain amount of shame and doubt. A sense of power and control needs to be bounded by a concern about the reactions of others and a concern for their approval. What is critical is that the child's sense of autonomy outweigh the sense of shame or doubt. The more we can encourage and support the toddler's growing sense of autonomy in a warm and accepting way, the more likely is that sense of autonomy to be solid and to overbalance the sense of shame and guilt. But we parents are human, too, and our occasional lapses into disappointment and frustration can contribute to the modicum of shame and doubt that are essential to balance a toddler's growing sense of autonomy.

Before turning to some examples of miseducation in the domain of autonomy, some other areas of motor development need to be described. For although Freud focused upon toilet training as the significant area of motor training for later personality development, Erikson suggests that all forms of motor training are involved in the determination of the balance of autonomy versus shame and doubt.

Other Motor Skills

It is useful to know the sequence of motor activities a young child can manage so that we can support these activities and encourage autonomy. At two years, for example, most children have sufficient motor coordination to enable them to scribble (preferably with a crayon), cut gashes in paper with a pair of blunt child's scissors, and pile four or five blocks into a tower. At this age, children can also string beads or spools on a shoelace and can begin to use a spoon and fork, although with a lot of spilling. At the same time, children at this age are not really interested in dressing themselves, in part because they lack the motor control. The introduction of Velcro into children's clothing may make it easier for younger children to participate in dressing themselves.

While it is important for us to recognize and encourage children's efforts in these domains, it is also important to take a light attitude toward children's successes and failures. Motor skills take time to learn, and we should not get upset if children spill a bit of food while trying to feed themselves. Certainly, if children only throw the food, that is another matter. But if they are really trying to get the job done, then we should support the endeavor and not worry too much about the spills. That is the way to encourage autonomy.

By age three, children have made much progress in motor ability, although children differ widely among themselves. If given the opportunity, most children of this age can copy a rough circle with a pencil and build a tower of more than five blocks. In addition, they can set a child-sized table if they are told how to do it, can feed themselves with a fork, help feed the family pet, and wipe up spilled things. Children of this age are eager and willing helpers, and allowing them to help is another way in which we can encourage a healthy sense of autonomy.

As adults, we sometimes forget that some of young children's difficulties in motor skills derive from the fact that most things in the household, from doorknobs, chairs, and tables to knives, forks, glasses, and plates are designed for adult-sized hands and adult-strength muscles. Maria Montessori recognized this when she introduced child-sized chairs and tables into her classes for preschool children. We can help the child learn self-help skills by such methods as having hooks or pegs at a child-sized level for the child to hang things on (items of clothing with loops for hanging are the easiest for this age group). We can make the bathroom more accessible to the young child if we have a nontippable stool or box for the child to stand on, and his or her own towel and washcloth with a special place to hang them.

It is necessary to say again that children are just learning these skills, so it is important not to force them. Children like the independence and autonomy of self-care, but sometimes they may get a little frightened of their newfound autonomy and may want to be looked after by the parent. These are usually just temporary regressions, which we should accept with good humor and with the recognition that we adults sometimes skip making the bed, shaving, or doing the dishes. Growing up, becoming independent and autonomous, is fun and exciting, but sometimes it gets a little scary, too, and it is good to know that parents are there as backup.

The important thing, as I have tried to suggest, is to find a healthy middle ground between doing everything for children and doing nothing for them and expecting them to cope with the adult-sized world. The intermediate, autonomy-strengthening approach is to expect children to engage in self-help activities but to make these activities more accessible to children by down-sizing the materials, or by breaking the skill down into smaller, more doable components whenever this is possible.

Motor Miseducation

At the heart of motor miseducation is the belief that if you start a child earlier in a particular motor skill, the child will have an advantage over children who begin learning that skill at a later age. The research simply does not support this assumption. John Watson, for example, was able to condition a baby to be toilet-trained between the age of six and eight weeks with the aid of suppositories![7] But in all such cases of early bowel and bladder training, it turns out that it is the parent, not the child, who is trained.[8] Furthermore, such early conditioned training breaks down when the child's voluntary participation is required.[9] (What such early training does to the child's sense of trust and autonomy is not hard to imagine.)

Similar conclusions can be drawn from two studies of identical twins. In these studies, one of each pair of twins was taught a motor skill, such as stair-climbing or cube manipulation, while the other twin was not. In both studies, the untrained twin learned the skill more easily when confronted with it at a later age. After the second twin had learned the skill, there were no differences between the twin who had learned the skill early and the one who had learned it late.[10] Training is important, too, of course, but it is much more effective and efficient when it is introduced when the child is physically ready than when it is not.

I would like to relate a personal footnote to one of these twin studies—to the study of the twins Johnny and Jimmy by Myrtle McGraw. A couple of years ago I was at a luncheon during a psychiatric meeting and was seated next to a distinguished psychiatrist who was being honored at the meeting. Knowing of my interest in the effects of hurrying, he told me an interesting story. He had seen the twins that McGraw had studied some years after the investigation. The twin who had been trained early, he told me, was quite different from the untrained twin. The trained twin was overly dependent on adults for direction and guidance, whereas the untrained twin demonstrated considerable autonomy.

The evidence regarding the motor training of young children, then, clearly indicates that a certain amount of maturation is essential for effective and efficient learning to occur. And yet this evidence is repeatedly ignored by those who are selling early motor skill training to parents. Not only is such skill training of no value, it also puts the child's sense of autonomy at risk. Consider the following instruction given to parents in a book about teaching infants to swim:

> Flipping is the procedure by which the baby turns from his stomach to his back—i.e., from a face-down to face-up position in the water. Begin by pulling the baby from the steps towards you and getting him in a floating glide. Then standing directly in front of the baby, hold his head between both your hands. Gently rotate the baby's head until his body follows through to a complete flip over on his back. The thing most instructors have trouble with here is keeping the baby's head level with the water throughout the rotation. Don't lift the baby's head out of the water: simply turn his head from face down to face up. The instant the baby is on his back, pick him up. Remember we don't want him to think about being on his back yet.
>
> As always, repeat this drill quickly, with occasional hugs in between.[11]

I can't speak for anyone else, but just reading those instructions gave me the shivers. Such procedures, I have to believe, must surely challenge the infant's sense of attachment and trust, not to mention the beginning sense of autonomy. Here is a good case of miseducation, where a child is put at risk not only for physical illness (middle-ear infections, autoasphyxiation, and diarrhea), but also for long-lasting personality damage—for no reason.

Programs designed to teach three- and four-year-olds to ski, play tennis, do karate, and engage in gymnastics miseducate young children in a somewhat different way. Most of the motor activities children spontaneously engage in do not require much in the way of instruction. Eating with a spoon and fork, scribbling, setting the table, and so on, can be accomplished almost completely through imitation, a natural way for children to learn motor skills. But to learn to ski, or to play tennis, or do ballet, the child has to receive instruction. Imitation plays a role, but the skills are too complex for imitation itself to be of much use. Very young children subjected to such instruction are in danger of learning to be overly dependent upon adults for guidance and direction. Their budding sense of autonomy is thus put at risk for no purpose. As shown by the twin studies discussed above, this danger is avoided, and the skills can be learned more effectively and efficiently, when they are taught at a later, more appropriate age.

The first three years of life are critical for the child's attainment of a healthy sense of trust and autonomy stronger than the sense of mistrust, shame, and doubt. Miseducation in the form of early instruction puts the child's sense both of trust and of autonomy at risk for no demonstrable gain of any kind. It is only the purveyors of athletic instruction for infants and young children who profit from such programs.

6

Initiative and Belonging Versus Guilt and Alienation

INITIATIVE IS INDIVIDUAL; belonging is social. The fourth and fifth years of life—when children are three and four—are witness to psychosocial crises for each of these potentials. Erik Erikson describes this period as one that determines whether the child's sense of *initiative* will be strengthened to an extent greater than the sense of *guilt*. And because the child is now interacting with peers, this period is also critical in the determination of whether the child's sense of *"belonging"* will be greater than the sense of *alienation*.

As with earlier crises, parents play a crucial role in how these crises are resolved. But because many children now spend at least some time in out-of-home programs, the child's experiences in these programs also contribute to the resolution of these crises. It is during this age period, then, that miseducation outside the home can begin to contribute to negative as well as positive resolutions of psychosocial crises.

INITIATIVE VERSUS GUILT

Erikson describes the crisis of initiative in his usual elegant prose:

There is in every child at every stage a new miracle of unfolding, which constitutes a new hope and a new responsibility for all. Such is the sense and pervading quality of initiative. The criteria for all these senses and qualities are the same: a crisis, more or less beset with fumbling and fear, is resolved, in that the child suddenly seems to "grow together" both in his person and in his body. He appears "more himself," more loving, relaxed and brighter in his judgment, more activated and activating. He is in fresh possession of surplus energy which permits him to forget failures quickly to approach what seems desirable (even if it also seems uncertain and even dangerous) with undiminished and more accurate direction. Initiative adds to autonomy the quality of undertaking, planning and "attacking" a task for the sake of being active and on the move whereas before self-will, more often than not, inspired acts of defiance or, at any rate, protested independence.[1]

Although the child's sense of initiative can be observed in many different domains, it becomes particularly prominent in the child's increasingly more proficient verbal interactions. Because such interactions are also occasions for miseducation, as well as for healthy education, it seems reasonable to focus upon these interactions in describing the crisis of initiative versus guilt.

Development of Verbal Interactions

We know now that language interaction between parent and child is a very complex process that goes way beyond the words that are spoken.[2] There is between parent and child a complex and total language environment that includes intonation, facial expression, patterning, and rhythm—all of which communicate to the child and all of which the child learns to use in return. Learning a first language is much more than learning vocabulary and grammar: it involves learning to be a human individual and to relate to another person; it means learning the ways of thinking and feeling peculiar to the people who speak that language; it means learning a culture.

During the first year of life, the infant begins to use what Jean Piaget[3] terms "signs" and "signals" as a first step in the attainment of language. A sign is part of what it signifies, a part of a whole. After only a few months of life, for example, the infant can distinguish the mother's voice from other voices. The voice can be a sign of the "whole" mother when the infant hears but does not see her. When the infant orients to the mother's voice even when she is out of the room, the infant is responding to a sign.

A "signal" is a more arbitrary representation. Suppose that the baby's room is on the second floor and that there is a squeaky step on the staircase. Every time the mother comes up the stairs to feed her baby, she is preceded by the sound of the squeaking stair. After a few months of being exposed to this association of squeaky stair/mother's breast, the baby will start to orient to the sound of the squeaky stair, and will even initiate sucking movements, before the mother appears.

During the second year, the toddler gives evidence of a new level of symbolic ability—namely, the ability to use language creatively. During the second year of life, the infant learns to reproduce the sounds of the language spoken by the parents and begins to reproduce a few words. Such single words, however, often represent a whole sentence: "up" means "pick me up"; "milk" means "I want some milk." This is the first hallmark of the symbolic system, because the child is using language "creatively." As parents, for example, we do not speak to infants in single-word sentences, so their use of single-word sentences is creative and not imitative.

It is the toddler's ability to create new uses for symbols, and even new symbols, that separates human infants from those of any other species. Although some investigators who have taught chimpanzees sign languages claim that these animals have created new symbols, the matter is still very much in dispute.[4] What is not in dispute is how easily and readily young children create their own new words. The creation and use of such words is the single most important index that the child has indeed acquired the symbolic system.

Over the years I have gathered a collection of words that children have created. These words are attempts by a child to convey some general concept the child has formed with a word. Sometimes the concept is a common one, but the child does not know the word and makes up one. Sometimes, however, the toddler cuts the world up a little differently from the way adults do, so that there is no word for the new concept and, undaunted, the toddler creates a new word by a kind of approximation process. Here is a list of some of the words that young children have created to signify either familiar concepts or concepts that they themselves have created:

"Furry sheet"	Blanket
"Daddy's work purse"	Briefcase
"Choo-choo bird"	Airplane
"Stocks"	Mommy's stockings, daddy's socks
"Mouthbrow"	Mustache

When children use these words, they don't bother to define them because they assume that everybody knows exactly what they mean. Sometimes these words become part of the family vocabulary, and children grow up using such a word as "stocks" for stockings and socks without realizing that the word is not generally used in that way. It is the creation and use of new symbols, then, which is the distinctive mark of the symbolic system and which places the child who attains it on a new plane of mental functioning.

Once children become sufficiently proficient in language,

they begin to use it to interact with adults in new ways. Initially, during the early stages of language acquisition, the child uses language to make the internal world external, to express his or her needs, wants, fears, and pleasures. During the fourth and fifth years of life, however, the child begins to use language about the world to make the external world internal. The prime vehicle for this new use of language is the question. Children's questions, however, are not merely attempts at information-getting, they are also expressions of children's budding sense of initiative. Children's questions thus provide an arena for the determination of whether the children's sense of initiative will become stronger than their sense of guilt.

Children's Questions

Four- and five-year-old children are notorious question-askers, and children's questions represent an effort at intellectual initiative as well as an attempt to take the social initiative in interacting with adults. If we respond appropriately to the children's questions, we provide them with the sense that the effort and anxiety involved in taking the intellectual and social initiative are worthwhile. We thus provide children with the foundation for taking the initiative as older children or as adults. On the other hand, if we ignore the meaning and the importance of children's questions, we not only lose an opportunity to encourage social and intellectual initiative, we may also contribute to children's associating curiosity with a sense of guilt. At the same time, a little guilt is healthy, and if we slip up sometimes in answering a child's questions, that may provide the bit of guilt necessary to balance an overweening sense of initiative.

When we answer children's questions, the first thing to remember is not to be deceived by the vocabulary and syntax. We must always keep in mind that young children's verbal skills far outpace their conceptual knowledge. Preschoolers sound much brighter and more knowledgeable than they really are, which is why so many parents and grandparents are so sure their progeny are gifted and super-bright. Because children's questions sound so mature and sophisticated, we are tempted to answer them at a level of abstraction far beyond the child's level of comprehension. That is a temptation we should resist.

An example will help illustrate what I mean. While spending some time in a nursery school, I talked with a five-year-old I had seen on several occasions who suddenly asked me, "What is your true identity?" After my initial shock I began to wonder whether I might have misjudged the mental level of this age group. I was feeling a little guilty, too, since ostensibly I was there to do a study, when in fact I was there to observe a troubled child. How in the world had I blown my cover? My training as a psychologist (always answer a tough question with a question) again stood me in good stead, and I replied, "What do you mean, my 'true identity'?" He looked at me and said, "Well, I watched 'Superman' last night, and Clark Kent is Superman's true identity."

Children's question-asking can be misleading in other ways. One day one of my sons, then of preschool age, asked me, "Daddy, why does the sun shine?" I was tempted to give him a scientific explanation about the relationship of heat and light. But I reflected on what Piaget[5] had written about this age period and the fact that preschool children are primarily interested in the "purpose" of things rather than an explanation of how they work, so I answered, "To keep us warm, and to make the grass and the flowers grow." Such an answer is truthful in a certain sense and yet speaks to the true import of the child's question.

Some parents might object, however, that such an approach is "coddling" children and that they should be given the scientific explanation even if they do not understand it, because at least the children hear the right words, and the struggle to understand is a step toward full understanding later. The correct scientific answer challenges children's intelligence and encourages curiosity, they claim. My answer would, in my own terms, "miseducate" them.

These parents clearly have a point. The question of intellectual challenge is a legitimate one, but we have to distinguish between "intelligent" and "unintelligent" challenge. An "intelligent" challenge would be an answer that is enough beyond the child's level of comprehension to encourage an effort at understanding that can succeed in whole or in part. An "unintelligent" challenge is one that presents the child with information such that, no matter how much effort the child expends, no understanding will result. Unintelligent challenge is frustrating and discourages initiative and encourages guilt (for not understanding).

To illustrate, I might have said, "Rick, light is a form of energy that is given off when some atoms break down and release electrons," which would have left him dazed and dazzled but no more knowledgeable than he was before. Because such an answer is far beyond the child's level of comprehension, it is an example of unintelligent challenge. Or I might have said, "Rick, hot things give off light." This is an answer he could grasp but not fully understand. The problem with this answer is that it prompts another question: "Why do hot things give off light?" This brings us back to the fact that the child is really asking, "For what purpose does the sun shine?" and really will not be satisfied until an answer in terms of purpose is given.

When we answer a child's questions at the level of purpose, at the level at which they are asked, we can still challenge the child intellectually. The child knows that the sun shines and that it is warm, but might not have thought that it helps the flowers, trees, and grass to grow. In this way we respond to the child's true intent and also expand the child's understanding of the function of sunlight in a manner and at a level that the child can understand. Likewise, a child who knows some animals and some shapes can be intelligently challenged by learning additional animals and additional shapes. In general, we can challenge a child more by horizontal enrichment (by elaborating on what the child already knows) than by vertical acceleration (by introducing totally new and abstract concepts).

There are a couple of other suggestions for answering children's questions that will reinforce children's sense of intellectual and social initiative. First, if you are stuck and really don't know what to answer, ask the child! Most children already have, or think they have, the answer to the question they are asking. After all, the child is asking the question as much to initiate interaction as to get an answer and is more than happy to reply. It is important, moreover, to accept the child's answer regardless of how farfetched it seems. If the child, for example, says, "Because it wants to," we might reply, "Oh, that's interesting, and I'll bet it helps the grass and the flowers to grow, too." Accept the child's answer as an expression of opinion, not a statement of fact. The worst thing we can do is to say, "Oh no, that's wrong; the sun isn't alive. What is the matter with you!" Our aim in answering or responding to children's questions is to encourage intellectual and social initiative, not discourage it.

A somewhat different issue arises when children ask questions about sensitive topics such as sex and death. Again, it is important to remember that children's language ability far outstrips their conceptual understanding, and we have to be cautious about not reading into a child's language more than is there. The following story illustrates the point. A seven-year-old came home from school one day and asked his father, "What does sex mean?" The father, a little taken aback, decided it must be time to tell his son about the birds and the bees. After the father's embarrassed presentation he asked,

"Okay, do you understand?" His son replied, "Yeah, sure, but I still don't know which box to check on the test form where it says 'Sex, M or F.'"

Children's awareness of sexual intercourse is rudimentary at best; they are really not interested in, nor can they fully understand, sexual activity at that level. Most often, when preschoolers ask questions about sex, it is because they have heard someone, usually older children, talking about it in hushed tones that suggest it is something special, secret, or bad, or all three. It is the way the word is talked about and used that excites young children's curiosity, not the meaning of the words themselves. With sexual questions, we are best advised to ask children just what it is they mean by the words they are using.

In talking with young children about sexual matters, we need to be simple and straightforward and to call a penis a penis and to avoid analogies and complex explanations. When, for example, a child asks where babies come from, it really doesn't help the child to hear that they come from the hospital. We can say, "The baby grows in Mommy's stomach and then comes out to be with us." My sense is that that is as far as we need to go with young children and that any further explanation is likely to be confusing or upsetting. If children push further, we can, again, ask for their own explanation and leave it at that.

With respect to death, preschool children cannot grasp the concept in the same way adults do. It is for them a kind of going away from which you can return. To understand death in the biological sense of the termination of life requires an elementary grasp of the concept of biological life, which most children do not acquire until about the age of eight or nine. For example, when my youngest son was four, we found a dead bird, which I put in a small plastic bag and placed in the trash can. My son watched the whole procedure but said nothing. Several days later, however, he asked me, "Why do we bury people in the ground?" At first, I didn't make any connection with the incident of several days before and was a bit startled. Again following my established practice, I asked him in return, "Why shouldn't we bury them in the ground?" He replied, "Well, if we put them in the trash can they wouldn't get so dirty and it would be easier for them to get out again." For Rick, as for most preschoolers, death was not a permanent but a temporary condition that could be rectified.

If children ask questions about death in the abstract, it is well to turn the question back upon them and find out what answer they have formed for themselves. A different situation emerges when there has been a death in the family such as that of a grandparent. In such cases it is well to be simple and direct with children. We can say something like "Grandpa died and we love him and will miss him very much." It is best to avoid causal explanations that can give children wrong ideas. If we say that "Grandpa died because he was sick," children may believe that they will die when they get sick. Or if we say, "God loved him and God took him," children may become frightened that God will love them so much that He will take them as well.

Preschoolers' questions, to be sure, are but one of the ways in which young children try to show initiative. I have emphasized them here in part because, as adults, we have a tendency to ignore them or to dismiss them with some phrase such as "You will understand when you are older." In fact, however, as I have tried to show, children's questions are an attempt to strengthen their sense of intellectual and social initiative. We need, therefore, to encourage questions even if we do nothing more than ask for children's own answers.

BELONGING VERSUS ALIENATION

By four years of age, children are becoming interested in peers and peer-group play and begin talking about "my friend." Although the sense of social "belonging" is present from the beginning of life, the three-to-four-year-old period seems to be critical in the determination of the child's later sense of social integration or alienation. A child who does not develop a strong sense of belonging during this period may develop a sense of alienation that will later make it difficult for the person to become an active group member and make it more likely that he or she will be something of a loner. Before turning to the practices at home and at school that encourage a sense of belonging, we need to look at some of the dimensions of belonging and at some of the "natural" challenges to this sense. These challenges are not miseducation; they are natural or unavoidable challenges to the child's sense of belonging.

Dimensions of the Sense of Belonging

Although children acquire their first sense of belonging in interactions with their parents, the sense of belonging to the peer group emerges gradually during the preschool years. Jean Piaget observed[6] that young children of three years or so engage in what he called "parallel play," in which they play side by side but not with each other. Their conversations are parallel as well. One child may be talking about his trip to the market, while the other may be talking about the tower she is building. At this stage, a sense of belonging is hardly more than the sense of being in the company of another child.

At the next stage, usually at age four, children begin to engage in what Piaget called "cooperative play." In such play the children genuinely interact with one another in the sense that they take turns using a material and that they are truly talking "to" rather than "at" one another. Piaget attributes the emergence of cooperative play to the child's beginning capacity to take the other child's point of view. It is the young child's beginning ability to put himself or herself in another child's place that enables the child not only to play cooperatively but also to be empathetic with the other child's experience (say, when a child is hurt) when that experience is different from their own.

The child's sense of belonging depends not only upon the level of mental ability, but upon other characteristics as well. In this respect, the sense of belonging is like some of the Erikson potentials that have their crisis period at later periods of life. Though the resolution of these crises is affected by the child's early experience, other factors also determine the outcome. The same is true for the child's sense of belonging; although the sense of belonging to the family is critical to the general sense of belonging, so, too, is the child's sense of being accepted into the peer group.

At all age levels, the child's acceptance into the peer group seems associated with the child's friendliness and outgoingness: children who are open, friendly, and thoughtful of others are more apt to be liked and accepted by their peers than are children who are not friendly or open. It is also true that brighter children tend to be more popular than less bright children, and this appears to hold true for children at different socioeconomic levels and from different ethnic backgrounds.[7]

Physical appearance seems to play a role in peer acceptance as well. Bigger and huskier children are likely to be more accepted than smaller, skinnier children, and attractive children are likely to be more liked and accepted than less attractive children. Among girls good-looking—but not too good-looking—children are the most liked and accepted. Birth order may also play a role. Firstborn children tend to be more competitive and anxious than later-borns and are thus a little less likely to be accepted by peers. Last-born and only children are often likable and easily accepted into the group; they have not been replaced in the family structure and thus tend to be secure and positive in their outlook, characteristics that make for peer acceptance and a sense of belonging.[8]

Family characteristics also contribute to children's acceptance and approval by peers. In general, children who are popular with their peers come from families in which aggression and antisocial behavior are discouraged and cooperation is rewarded; there is little unnecessary frustration and punishment is minimal, and the children are liked and appreciated and are told this by their parents. Put differently, parenting practices that encourage children's sense of belonging to the family also facilitate their acceptance by the group and thus the sense of peer-group belonging.

Challenges to the Attainment of Belonging

It is important to emphasize that a child can acquire a healthy sense of belonging in the home and that such a sense of belonging does not require nursery school or day-care attendance. What is important is that the parents begin to include the children in their activities when this is possible. Taking children along to the store, or having them help by doing simple chores such as shelling peas or handing a parent tools when the parent is fixing something, encourages children's sense of belonging and discourages any sense of alienation.

One of the reasons divorce is so hard on young children is that it comes at just the time when the child needs to establish this sense of belonging, particularly to the family group. If the family is broken apart at this time, it is hard for the young child to strengthen a sense of belonging because what one belongs to is not clear. Whatever the custody arrangements, the family unit, the prime basis of the child's sense of belonging, is no longer intact.

This is not to say that couples should at all costs avoid divorce when their children are four or five years old. Life doesn't work that way. But if we recognize the importance of this period for the child's sense of belonging, we can help construct a broader unit for the child to belong to. This is relatively easy when there is a considerable extended family —grandparents, uncles, aunts, and cousins. Frequent visits with accepting extended-family members during this critical period will help the child acquire a sense of belonging that will outweigh the sense of social alienation.

The age at which children are most sensitive to acquiring a healthy sense of belonging is also the period during which a sibling may be brought into the family. If too much attention is paid to the new baby, the older sibling may feel pushed out and alienated. A four- or five-year-old child may feel this way even when parents make great efforts not to neglect the older child and to involve him or her in the baby's care. At such times we have to be persistent in our verbalizations of love and caring and in our attempts to include the young child in our activities. If we simply accept the child's sense of being left out and don't bother to keep trying to involve him or her, we may encourage the child's sense of alienation.

Another challenge to the child's sense of belonging is attendance in an out-of-home program. Sometimes a child will have difficulty in becoming a group member because of problems at home. For example, a young patient of mine who had been "spoiled" by his parents' lavish attention and overindulgence became aggressive and hostile at his nursery school after his baby sister was born. His sense of alienation at home caused him to engage in actions at school that furthered his sense of alienation and inhibited his sense of belonging. It did have the desired effect of getting him sent home from school to his parents, whose anger and resentment reinforced his sense of alienation. Such vicious circles have to be broken with professional help.

Some children, it must be said, move into the stage of belonging and alienation at a somewhat later age than the average child. Such children often play quite happily by themselves or with a sibling but are quite uncomfortable in groups. With such children, waiting six months to a year (when this is possible) usually resolves the problem. When it is necessary to put such children into a group setting before they are ready, it is helpful if the care-givers can allow the children to be in a quiet place and excused from group activities until they feel more comfortable in the situation.

So far we have talked about some of the "natural" challenges that may interfere with children's attainment of a healthy sense of belonging. Now we must look at the practices that, both at home and at school, will encourage children to attain a sense of belonging that is stronger than their sense of alienation. Again, it is important to recall that a certain degree of alienation is important. Too great a sense of belonging might produce a kind of automatic conformity to the group, which is not healthy, either. A certain amount of alienation makes us a little cautious about going along with the group tide.

Frames

The major way in which children acquire a sense of belonging is through learning a repertoire of what the late sociologist/anthropologist Erving Goffman[9] called "frames." In Goffman's usage, frames are repetitive social situations with their own rules, expectations, and understandings. For example, the preschool activity known as "Show and Tell" is a frame. In some nursery schools, the day begins with the children sitting in a circle and each child telling or showing something that has happened to him or her since the group met last. In this frame, the children learn that they must sit in the circle, that each child takes a turn, and that children who are not talking must listen to the child who is. In this case, the frame rules are set by the teacher, who also enforces them by speaking to a child who is violating the rules of the frame. As children become well entrenched in frames, they may enforce them themselves by complaining about a child who is not behaving according to the frame—"He pushed me!"

Young children learn an enormous number of frames, and it is the facility in social situations and the social awareness that the possession of such frame knowledge bestows that are critical to the sense of belongingness. Put differently, a sense of belonging derives, in part at least, from knowing how to operate in social situations.

The learning of frames is a complicated and time-consuming affair. And like other facets of development, there is a regular sequence in which frames must be learned. An infant, for example, must learn eating and playing frames before learning "family meal" and peer-group "game" frames. Children can be miseducated when they are taught frames inappropriate to their level of development. Before we consider the abuse of frames, we need to review their healthy, age-appropriate attainments.

Consider the number and variety of frames preschool children must learn: getting up, eating, going to the store, going to Grandpa and Grandma's, going to the doctor, playing with friends, parties, holidays, and so on. Each frame has its own set of rules, expectations, and understandings. Children must learn not only the frame rules, but also how to cope with frame switches and frame clashes. Such learning taxes the abilities of children and the patience of parents.

To illustrate the complexity of even a simple frame, consider the "eating dinner" frame. Some of the rules to be learned include: you must wash your hands before you eat; you must wait for everyone to be seated before you start to eat; you must keep your mouth closed and not talk with your mouth full; you must not leave the table without permission until everyone is ready to leave. The "going to bed" frame is equally elaborate: you must get into your pajamas, brush your teeth, say good night to Mommy and Daddy, and (depending upon the family) say your prayers.

Once acquired, frames have a very compelling quality, so that children often become quite upset if the frame rules are not followed. Children are not so much creatures of habit as they are devotees of frames. One reason, for example, that children are so touchy about words being left out of a story that they have heard many times is that leaving a word out breaks the frame, and frame violations trouble children. It is a breaking of the order on which they begin to depend for security in a changing and often frightening world.

For us as parents, awareness of frames helps us to handle certain situations better than we might if we were not aware of the frame aspect of socialization. First of all, it is important to state the frame rules and, more often than not, repeat them. Usually we do this automatically: "It is eight o'clock and time for you to go to bed. Put on your pajamas and don't forget to brush your teeth." But sometimes we may not verbalize all the parts of the frame we expect the child to learn, but yet we get upset if the child doesn't do what he or she was supposed to do. If a child is not following the frame rules, the first thing to do is to make sure that we have verbalized all the parts of the frame. Sometimes children have problems with frames because the rules have not been clearly verbalized, or because we have been inconsistent in expressing them.

One of the problems young children have is "switching" frames. We sometimes misread this reluctance to switch frames as a dislike of the frame itself, and this can be puzzling or distressing. Suppose a child is busy working on a coloring book and we invite him or her to go with us to the store, an outing the child usually enjoys. But the child is reluctant to go. The reluctance, however, comes not so much from not wanting to go as from not wanting to switch frames. We can all empathize with the child's situation. When one is sitting relaxed and comfortable in knock-about clothes on a Sunday afternoon, it takes a special effort to get dressed up and go out, even though we really do want to go to the restaurant or party. Frame-switching is always a wrench.

If we recognize this, we can help children switch frames with greater ease and less pain. The rule is always to alert children in advance that a frame switch is coming and to encourage them to finish the activity in question. A nursery school teacher who had been a flight attendant in a former life had a neat way of doing this with her charges. When she was preparing them for a major frame switch such as going out into the play yard, she would say, "Okay, children, we are coming in for a landing. Put your trays away, your brushes in the bottles, and fasten your seat belts. We will be going outside at eleven hundred hours." Alerting children five or ten minutes ahead of time that a frame switch is coming does much to ease the transition.

Sometimes, of course, children may be ready for a frame switch before we are, and we have to be sensitive to this situation as well. In one nursery school I visited, a young intern was reading to a group of preschoolers. After about ten minutes they began to squirm in their chairs, and as the intern read on, the squirming was accompanied by looking around, poking, and talking, all non-frame activities. But the intern droned on, impervious to the children's readiness to move on to a new frame. For the truth was that he was into his adult frame, namely, that when you read a story to children you have to finish it at one sitting!

It is important, then, not only to prepare children for frame switches, but also to be alert to children's readiness to switch frames before we are ready. The point is that young children process material and information at different rates than we adults do. Sometimes they are slow when we want to go fast, and sometimes fast when we want to go slow. Sometimes, of course, children must learn to slow their pace to ours. They have to learn to remain at the dinner table until everyone is ready to leave. And we must sometimes adjust to their frames when they have tired of an activity before we have. If we are sensitive to frame differences and frame similarities, it makes our lives and those of our children much easier. It also contributes in important ways to the child's sense of belonging.

Frames are part of the "hidden curriculum" of education.

A major finding of the Head Start programs[10] was that children who had been in Head Start classes as preschoolers were less likely than non–Head Start children of comparable backgrounds to be in special classes. Apparently, one of the important things Head Start children learn is the frames that allow a child to function in a school setting, where most of the frames are carried over from middle-class family life. By learning the appropriate frames, low-income children are enabled to acquire a sense of peer-group belonging that keeps them in school. Low-income children who do not acquire these frames in their early years may develop a sense of alienation which can contribute to their dropping out of school later.

The Abuse of Frames

Because frames are so important to the child's acceptance and sense of belonging, both within the family and at school, anything which interferes with the child's acquisition of frames or which encourages the learning of wrong frames constitutes miseducation. A parent who is following teaching procedures such as those suggested by the Engelmanns—

> Isolate the object
> Name the object
> Require the child to repeat the name
> Require the child to point to the object
> Require the child to name the object as you point

—is teaching the child not only the names of objects but also a very specific and very rigid learning frame. That frame includes the ideas that the infant must pay attention to the parent's instructions, that there is a "right" and a "wrong" response, and that "right" responses are "good" while "wrong" responses are "bad." A child who acquires this frame at an early age may become overly dependent upon adult direction and overly inhibited about initiating learning on his or her own. Equally important, the child can come to have too strong a sense of belonging, based on the idea that one can belong only if one conforms totally to the parental (and, later, teacher and peer-group) frames.

A major problem with most of the programs meant to teach young children academic skills is that they also teach the children frames in which acceptance and belonging have to be purchased at the price of blind conformity. This puts children's healthy sense of belonging, buffered by a balancing sense of alienation and individualism, at risk. And again, since there is no evidence that such early instruction, or the frames in which they are embedded, have any long-term benefits for children, their healthy sense of belonging is put at risk for no good purpose.

The years of four to five are critical for children's attainment of a healthy sense of initiative and a healthy sense of belonging, which have lifelong consequences. An individual who has acquired a healthy sense of initiative will welcome challenges and undertake new projects without the debilitating sense of guilt that handicaps those who move into adulthood with a weak sense of initiative. Likewise, the child who acquires a healthy sense of belonging will be prepared to be a productive as well as an independent group member who is neither overly conforming to nor overly alienated from the group's goals.

Helping children to acquire initiative and a sense of belonging is not difficult, and requires only that we accept the child's strengths and also limitations. We encourage initiative by answering children's questions at the level at which they were asked, or by encouraging children to answer their own questions. In the same way we encourage children's sense of belonging by being sensitive to situations where they may feel alienated (divorce, say, or the birth of a sibling) and by including them in our discussions and activities whenever this is possible.

We miseducate children in these domains when we become egocentric and place our own needs ahead of those of the children. While we all do this at times, it is only when we do it consistently that we are likely to ignore children's need to be listened to, to have their questions taken seriously and responded to in a thoughtful way. And it is when we become egocentric that we teach children frames that encourage conformity rather than cooperation. Ensuring that young children acquire a healthy sense of initiative and belonging is far more important than teaching them one or another academic skill.

7

Industry and Competence Versus Inferiority and Helplessness

F O R E R I K S O N , the elementary school period beginning at ages five and six is the crisis period in the determination of whether the child's sense of *industry* will become more established than the child's sense of *inferiority*. During the elementary school period, children have to learn the work habits that they will carry into adult life. Getting to school on time, paying attention, doing a good, neat job promptly are part of the sense of industry acquired at this time. On the other hand, if children experience excessive failure in efforts to meet the demands of schooling, their sense of inferiority, of being less able than others, will be enhanced.

Before the early school years, we can contribute to children's sense of industry by our praise and support of their successive achievements in motor, intellectual, and social skills. But we are no longer the only ones involved in our children's attainment of the sense of industry. The first years of school, the experiences children encounter in kindergarten and first grade, are of critical importance in determining whether the sense of industry will be stronger than the sense of inferiority. Again, a slight sense of inferiority is a necessary and healthy counterpoise to what might otherwise become an overly powerful sense of industry.

The child's sense of industry and of inferiority derive from social comparison. Our sense of our own industriousness depends in part upon a comparison of our own work and achievement with those of others. The same is true for inferiority: a sense of inferiority is always in reference to the achievements of other people.

In addition to comparing ourselves to others, we also evaluate ourselves, and such evaluations are what determine whether our sense of *competence* will be stronger than our sense of *helplessness*. Our sense of competence derives from a feeling of confidence in our knowledge, skills, and talents and our ability to put them into practice. Our sense of helplessness comes from a feeling of insecurity regarding our skills and knowledge and regarding our ability to put them to effective use. The early years of school, particularly at ages five and six, are critical in the determination of the long-term balance between our sense of competence and our sense of helplessness.

During the early years, we can contribute to children's budding sense of competence by encouraging their sense of trust, autonomy, initiative, and belonging, all of which contribute in a positive way to children's sense of security and self-confidence. While these early experiences are important, school experiences are also a major contributor to the balance between children's sense of competence and their sense of helplessness.

INDUSTRY VERSUS INFERIORITY

The school's contribution to a child's sense of industry is very much dependent upon the fit, or "match," between the modes of learning of young children and the curriculum. When educational practice is tuned to these modes of learning, then the children are successful and their sense of industry is supported and strengthened. If, however, the methods of instruction presuppose the modes of learning found only in older children, the young pupils are more likely to experience frustration and failure, which in turn contribute to a strong sense of inferiority.

We must review two modes of learning in young children which can contribute to a healthy sense of industry if properly mobilized, but which can contribute to a sense of inferiority if they are not.

Manipulative and Fundamental Learning

The learning of young children is *manipulative* and *fundamental* as opposed to the learning of older children and adults, which is *symbolic* and *derived*. For us as adults it is easy to take our immediate world of animate beings and inanimate objects for granted. We are so caught up in our symbolic worlds of future plans and projects, of past successes and failures, that the immediate world often seems secondary to what is to come or what has gone before. Even when we do concentrate upon the present, as in savoring a special dish or a fine wine, our pleasure comes as much from a sophisticated, experienced palate as from the food or wine itself. As we mature, each new experience is interpreted from generalizations of similar experiences in the past and anticipations of comparable experiences in the future.

For the young child, however, there is only the present, and each experience is fresh and unique. We all recall, I think, our first encounter with sweet corn, wild berries, or ice cream. Somehow the sweet corn we get as adults never tastes quite the same as it did when we were children, nor do the berries we buy at the store taste as good as those we picked in our neighbor's yard. To be sure, this is part nostalgia, part a matter of tired taste buds, but it is also a matter of the striking quality of a first experience with a taste treat.

Likewise, the color of the wallpaper, the changing pattern

of light and shadow in the nursery from morning to night, the gentle songs of birds, the machine rumble of cars and trucks, of airplanes and vacuum cleaners, are all new to the young child. So, too, are the smooth textures of plastic teething rings, the rough texture of the blanket, and the bristly texture of Daddy's beard when he kisses you before he shaves. Smells are no less a novelty. The smells of breakfast, lunch, and dinner are each different, as are the smells of Mommy's perfume and a pet's body odor. Some smells are unpleasant and make you wrinkle your nose and turn away.

Young children, then, learn through direct encounters with the immediate world of people and objects, through exploring these experiences with all their senses and combining these experiences to arrive at more complex and complete schemas, or elementary concepts of the furnishings of everyday life. This type of manipulative learning is a necessary prerequisite to the symbolic learning that will come later.

A simple research observation will help make this point. If young children are presented with a finger maze, a tabletop maze with grooves wide enough to permit a child to move a finger along the various paths, they will explore the maze with their fingers, retreat at the blind alleys, and eventually find the way out after some trial and error. If, however, you present the same maze to older children who have attained symbolic modes of learning, they explore the maze visually before they touch it, arrive at the solution symbolically, and then proceed to move their fingers along the correct path without error. After the age of six or seven, symbolic manipulation takes precedence over actual or manual manipulation.

The learning of a young child is also fundamental, rather than derived, as it will be later. Fundamental learning is what all young children in all parts of the world and in all of previous history have learned. Such learning is not derived from the learning and achievement of our society or culture; it is the kind of learning that is part of our animal heritage and that is basic to survival. Bad and good smells, sounds of security and safety, tastes of freshness and of something gone bad, textures that offer comfort and those that offer pain, as well as basic concepts of space, time, causality, and objects—all have to be acquired if the child is to survive.

The learning of older children is symbolic and derived. It is symbolic in that it involves written or spoken words and numbers, and it is derived because the symbols and concepts are those that have been created and handed down by the children's culture. To be sure, by the age of two, children begin to learn words and to acquire some derived concepts. The age period of three to six is an overlap one between manipulative-fundamental learning and symbolic-derived learning. But the general learning principle of this period is still the same: explore, manipulate, and conceptualize the object, quality, or relationship.

The fact that young children learn in manipulative and fundamental ways should be the basis of educational practice for this age group. When we provide rich and variegated materials that make extensive exploration and manipulation possible, we also encourage children's sense of industry. Providing the materials is only the starting point, however. Teachers trained in early-childhood education know how to help guide children's explorations and manipulations so that they can gain the most from these activities. The early-childhood teacher thus provides a model of systematic and organized exploration and manipulation that the child can incorporate. From such modeling the child acquires a sense that there is a system and direction to learning which becomes an important part of the child's sense of industry.

We miseducate young children when we ignore the manipulative and fundamental nature of their learning. When we push the first-grade curriculum into the kindergarten, we are imposing symbolic and derived learning experiences on children who, for the most part, are not ready for such experiences. The same negative consequences occur when children are promoted who are developmentally young for their age. In both cases, the results can have long-term negative consequences for children's sense of industry and their eventual school and vocational success. There is considerable evidence to support the negative effects of presenting formal instruction to children who are not yet equipped to learn in the symbolic and derived modes.

First of all, with respect to pushing formal instruction into kindergarten, some crosscultural data is instructive. In Denmark, formal reading instruction is not introduced until the second grade. Before that, children have a rich exploratory and manipulative language experience; they are read to and talked to, encouraged to dictate their own stories and learn sight words. Denmark has almost 100 percent literacy.[1]

In France, there is a state-mandated reading program that is begun in kindergarten. French children are thus exposed to formal instruction in reading at age five. In contrast to Denmark, France has some 30 percent of children with reading problems.[2] In Japan, formal instruction in reading is also begun early, but there are fewer reading problems than in France because the spelling is phonetic and thus eliminates some of the logical difficulties inherent in languages without totally phonetic spelling systems, such as French and English.[3] In a phonetic language, each symbol has one and only one sound attached to it, and thus learning this language is easier than learning a language where the same sound can be represented by different letters and the same letter can represent different sounds. In a sense, a phonetic language is to a nonphonetic, or only partially phonetic, language what a digital clock is to a regular clockface. Just as a child can tell time from a digital clock before telling time from a clockface, a child can learn to read a phonetic language before learning to read a nonphonetic language.

There is also evidence that individual children who are

exposed to formal instruction (symbolic and derived learning) too early experience both short-term and long-term negative effects. A number of studies have found that children who enter kindergarten early, before the age of five, are more likely to do poorly academically and to drop out of high school than children who are older than age five when they enter kindergarten.[4]

In a recent doctoral dissertation, McCarty[5] examined the effects of promoting and not promoting developmentally young (young for their age) kindergarten children to first grade. Her study is one of the few to look at the effects of nonpromotion over a long time interval. McCarty found that after eight years the nonpromoted youngsters were significantly ahead of the promoted youngsters in peer acceptance, classroom adjustment, and academic achievement. It is reasonable to assume that the nonpromoted children had acquired a healthier sense of industry than the promoted youngsters. Again, this is attributable to the exposure of the promoted youngsters to formal instruction before they left the manipulative and fundamental learning mode.

A caution has to be introduced here, however. While nonpromotion may have been a healthy educational practice in the past, it may not be so today. Several recent studies suggest that, in some schools at any rate, nonpromotion has become a social stigma with negative consequences for the child's self-concept, although it is still beneficial for academic achievement. This new effect of nonpromotion may reflect the new pressures on young children for academic achievement and their new awareness at an early age of the importance placed on academic achievement by parents and peers. This new data provides a good example of how the new "superkid" and "competent child" psychologies can have a negative effect upon what was once a healthy educational practice.[6]

The majority of kindergarten children are not ready for formal instruction involving the learning of symbolic rules and derived information. When such instruction is introduced at the kindergarten level, the children's sense of industry is put at risk, and the chances of their experiencing a heightened sense of inferiority are increased. And the evidence shows that children who have their sense of industry impaired at an early age are at risk for later school failure. When it comes to formal instruction, which requires symbolic and derived learning, earlier is not better.

Permeable Learning

The learning of young children is permeable in the sense that the categories of skills and subjects we use to organize learning and instruction for older children are really nonexistent for children below the age of six or seven. Young children do not organize their thinking and knowledge in subject-matter terms such as reading, math, science, and art. Rather, their thinking is organized around projects, activities, and frames. Each project, activity, or frame includes skills and information which at a later age might be grouped under one or another subject-matter category, but which for young children are part of a global whole.

An example of permeability may help make this mode of learning a little more concrete. Consider a group of four- and five-year-old children engaged in a common project such as making vegetable soup. Some children are peeling carrots, others are cleaning celery and green peppers, still others are pulling stems from cherry tomatoes, while the remaining youngsters are shelling peas. Once all of the vegetables are prepared, the teacher puts them in a pot on the stove, adds water and seasoning, and turns on the burner while the children look on.

What do the children learn from this activity? The children are learning social cooperation. Each is playing a contributing role in a common project from which all of the children will benefit. They will all get to eat the soup. They are learning the names, colors, and shapes of the vegetables, as well as the difference between peeled and unpeeled vegetables. They are learning to discriminate and label different degrees of consistency such as "crisp," "limp," and "soggy." They are also learning a lesson of physics and chemistry: boiling softens vegetables.

But that is not all the learning that takes place when children help in making soup. They are also learning about weights and measures as they follow a recipe directions regarding the weight or numbers of carrots, peas, and tomatoes to be put into the soup. They have to time the boiling and so learn something about clock time as well. In making soup, children learn a good deal about science, language, math, art, and social interaction, but without being aware of that fact. All they are aware of, or need to be aware of, is that they are having fun making soup.

When educational programs for young children appreciate the permeability of their learning and provide multiple projects, activities, and frames for children to employ their exploratory and manipulative skills, the programs foster the children's sense of industry. When children prepare soup, bake bread, create valentines for their mothers and friends, weave a paper basket to put Easter eggs in, or paint a mask for Halloween, they have learned many fundamental concepts, but they have also had an experience of bringing a task to completion with a product which is usable and which can be taken home and admired by parents. Such an achievement contributes much more to young children's sense of industry than does a grade on a work paper.

The permeable nature of young children's learning provides still another reason why the formal instruction of young children amounts to miseducation. Formal education presupposes instruction in specific skills such as reading and math, while the child's mind does not function within fixed categories at all; there is permeability everywhere. Young children may not attend to what is going on in the lesson for many different reasons. They may be caught up in trying to understand the words, when the teacher is intent upon phonics. I recall one child diagnosed as having a severe reading problem. It turned out that she could never get beyond the initial phrase of fairy tales: she was struggling to understand what "Once upon a time" meant, for she could not imagine herself being "upon" a time.

Sometimes the permeability of children's learning is recognized but is seen as something to be avoided. For example, as part of my research on visual perception, I wanted to study the perceptual development of limited-hearing children. Did the absence or limitation of hearing improve their perceptual abilities (the so-called compensation theory), or were their visual abilities impaired as well (the so-called correlation theory). To try and answer this question I got permission to test young children in a school for the deaf, and had a student who could both sign and speak as my assistant.

As is my usual practice, I arranged to spend some time in the classroom with the children I was going to test before I actually began the examination. In this way the children would have a chance to see me and to become familiar with my presence before we sat down to our task—it makes for a more comfortable interview. My classroom time with these children was, however, one of the most distressing school experiences I have ever had.

Let me say first that the school itself was extraordinarily beautiful. The building was a refurbished old mansion located on the shore of one of the Great Lakes, and had been donated to the school by a family that had had a deaf child. The rooms had high ceilings, beautiful woodwork, and large, wide windows of the European variety. But the splendor of the physical plant, and the well-kept lawns and flower beds, only served to intensify the distress I felt when I entered the classroom.

The first thing I noticed was that the walls were painted a stark white, not off-white softened by a tinge of yellow or beige. The starkness of the walls was accentuated by the emptiness of the room: there were no plants, no animals, no pictures on the walls, no toys or models or materials of any sort. In the middle of the room the teacher sat on a hard-backed chair with eight children sitting around her in smaller but equally hard-backed chairs. They were working on a lesson, and the teacher was finger-spelling to them while they followed her and the book in their laps.

I knew the philosophy of education that dictated this sort of classroom, but I had never seen it carried to this extreme before. The theory is that these children are easily distracted (their learning is permeable) and that in order to get them to concentrate on the lessons they need a dull and uninteresting environment. As I sat watching the children follow the exercise, a phrase kept running through my mind and I almost said it to the teacher. But I kept my silence. Later, when I had a chance to take a solitary walk around the grounds and was sure that I was out of earshot of the school, I shouted out what I had wanted to say in the classroom: "My God, these children are deaf—they are not dead!"

What is wrong with this educational philosophy is the same thing that is wrong with those who would instruct young children in single subjects: it ignores the way young children learn. Young limited-hearing children, like young hearing children, learn in a permeable way, not in a restricted fashion. Eliminating so much from the classroom eliminates much that a child might learn as well. Far from being distracted by rich environment of plants, animals, pictures, and materials, limited-hearing children no less than hearing children incorporate and work those experiences into whatever they are learning about. We can limit what we teach, but we cannot limit what children learn.

The negative effects of ignoring the permeability of young children's learning, and of teaching them isolated academic subjects, has been demonstrated in a couple of recent investigations. In one study, children who attended academic and nonacademic preschool programs were followed until age fifteen. Children who had attended the academic preschool (and were taught subjects rather than engaging in projects) were significantly more likely than the children who had attended the age-appropriate program to engage in delinquent actions as teenagers.[7] In another study it was found that low-income children who attended an academic preschool showed more aggression in elementary school than did comparable children who attended traditional day-care centers.[8] Aggressive acting out is often the expression of a sense of inferiority.

Educational practices that ignore the exploratory, fundamental, and permeable nature of young children's learning put their sense of industry at risk. Young children who move into later childhood and adolescence with an impaired sense of industry and heightened feelings of inferiority have been found to have more academic difficulty, to be more likely to drop out of school, and to be more aggressive than children who move into the later stages of childhood with a healthy sense of industry. Both the pupils and society pay a high price for the miseducation of young children.

COMPETENCE VERSUS HELPLESSNESS

Attaining a healthy sense of competence that is stronger than a sense of helplessness is also dependent, in part at least, upon the match between the school curriculum and the child's modes of learning. But a sense of competence derives from two other early-childhood learning modes that are increasingly ignored as the curricula and teaching methods from the higher grades are pushed down to first grade, kindergarten, and pre-kindergarten. While a small degree of feeling helpless is necessary to keep us from being overconfident, too much failure too early is liable to undermine this healthy balance.

The Structural Imperative

Psychologists generally distinguish between extrinsic (reward/punishment) and intrinsic (curiosity, self-esteem, pride) motivation. The structural imperative is one form of intrinsic motivation, a motivation that derives from children's need to realize an intellectual potential or mental structure. Young children's learning of language provides a good example of the structural imperative. Young children learn to speak first and foremost because they have the physical apparatus (tongue, vocal cords, lungs) as well as the brain structures that make language possible. The very use of this equipment provides the stimulation for its further use. The infant's babbling, for example, is the stimulus for further babbling. To be sure, as the child's language becomes more elaborate, it comes to serve other motives as well; but in its acquisition stages, language is an expression of the structural imperative.

In general, the structural imperative is most in evidence when a structure is in the process of formation. Once the structure is formed, the intrinsic structural imperative diminishes and other intrinsic or extrinsic motives serve to activate the utilization of the fully formed structure. For example, the structural imperative for learning language is generally gone by the age of eleven or twelve[9] and it takes an extrinsic motive (such as getting a college degree) to learn a foreign language thereafter. Young children, in contrast, learn a second language with great ease when it is spoken by those around them.

During the fifth and sixth years of life, children are attaining the new mental structure that Piaget terms "concrete operations." These operations, once attained, allow children to learn rules such as "When two vowels go walking, the first one does the talking"; they make it possible for children to grasp English phonics (that one and the same letter, say, *a*, can be sounded in different ways) and to understand the unit concept essential to an understanding of mathematical operations. Concrete operations are essential for a child to profit from formal instruction, but they are not acquired through formal instruction.

There are many evidences of the structural imperative associated with the attainment of concrete operations. For example, because concrete operations make possible the child's quantitative thinking, children during this period often seek out stimulation that will enhance and further their quantitative understanding. When one of my sons was at this stage, he would embarrass me by reading off the numbers as they ticked off on the taxi meter. He would also spontaneously practice his developing abilities and look for an audience as well: "Do you want to hear me count to a thousand?"

One of the reasons children like fairy tales is that such stories often provide stimulation for the child's developing quantitative faculty. Recall that in "Goldilocks and the Three Bears" there are degrees of size (bowls, chairs, beds) that are an important part of the story. In "The Three Little Pigs" the houses are of increasing degrees of strength and resistance to the wolf's huffing and puffing. And in "The Fisherman and His Wife" the wife wants bigger and bigger houses and honors until she ends up back in their little shack. Obviously, these stories appeal to young children for many reasons, but the quantitative stimulation is certainly one.

When we support and encourage children's structural imperative, we also strengthen their sense of competence in themselves and in their abilities. Answering a child's questions, for example, not only strengthens the child's sense of initiative but also provides stimulation for the language and mental abilities that support the child's sense of competence. And when we not only listen to children count but respond to their demands to give them verbal addition and subtraction problems, we are again providing stimuli for the structural imperative and support for children's sense of competence.

At home and at school, the attainment of concrete operations is facilitated by providing children with the materials that both nourish and exercise these developing operations. Materials such as an odd assortment of buttons that can be classified by color or size are one example. Graded series of blocks, sticks, or geometric forms that can be arranged according to increasing or decreasing size are also useful materials for the structural imperative. Unit materials such as beads or toy coins that can be counted provide another material that both nourishes and exercises children's emerging mental abilities. Children also have a structural imperative to write and, if allowed to do so without concern about correct spelling, will produce ingenious, and quite legible, "inventive spelling."

When the educational program for five- and six-year-olds is rich with such materials and the children are given ample time and thoughtful guidance in working with them, the structural imperative is supported and children acquire a healthy sense of competence in their own abilities. In contrast, children who are placed in formal instructional programs during this period are not given the materials and guidance they need to nourish and exercise their concrete operations. Rather, the formal instruction presupposes the very operations that are just in the process of formation. The result is a sense of frustration, a sense of being unable to cope, a sense of helplessness.

Helplessness can be learned,[10] and at least one investigator[11] suggests that some schools may increase children's vulnerability to learned helplessness by stressing performance goals (grades) rather than learning goals (skills, knowledge, and values). Although the failure to support the structural imperative is serious for all children, it is particularly so for intellectually gifted or talented youngsters. When the structural imperative of such children is not given the nourishment and opportunities for exercise and realization it needs, it is not only the child's loss but also society's. An example of a talented child whose structural imperative was given the appropriate guidance, support, and stimulation is given below:

> Dalit Warshaw was one of the winners of the 1984 BMI International Competition for student composers. Her winning four-piece composition was entitled "Fun Suite." At the time of the competition this suite had already been performed by the Rockland Suburban Orchestra, by the Denver Symphony Orchestra and had been broadcast on WQXR-FM. In addition to her composing talents Dalit is also a performing artist and several months before the competition she gave a solo piano recital in which she played Beethoven's Sonata in G Major and Mozart's Fantasia in D Minor. In 1984, when Dalit finished a winner in the BMI International Competition, she was nine years old!
>
> Here is how Lilian Kalir, a concert pianist, appraised Dalit's playing:
>
> "She's absolutely extraordinary," Lilian said. "Her creativity, her rhythm, her joy—it's artistry you can't learn. Her technique isn't even that good, but her sound is exceptional." And as for her original compositions Lilian Kalir said:
>
> "They'd be amazing even if they were done by listening to records and then imitating. But it's much more than that. The pieces are enormously, wildly imaginative. If I had a child like that I am not sure what I would do. You have to be terrified that you might do something wrong, that you might not support the gift properly."[12]

Dalit's gift appeared early and spontaneously. Her mother's "teaching" was a direct outgrowth of Dalit's interest and evidence of musical talent.

Dalit expressed interest in the piano even as a toddler, and when she reached three and a half, Ruti (her beautiful, Israeli-born mother who is also an accomplished pianist) began giving her lessons. It was soon apparent that she was a quick study. A year later, eager for an informed but objective opinion, Ruti convinced Nadia Reisenberg, a highly respected Juilliard faculty member and piano teacher, to hear Dalit play. Reisenberg was very encouraging, both to Dalit and to Ruti, who had been reluctant to continue teaching her own child. "Stay with it," Reisenberg told her. "Don't enroll her in a music school, because they will make her play like a robot."[13]

Reisenberg's concern about enrolling Dalit in a music school is just the one we are concerned with in this book. Not only would enrolling Dalit in formal instruction make her play like a robot, it might affect also her sense of competence. By giving her daughter the instruction she demanded, rather what the mother or a teacher decided she should have, Dalit's mother intuitively knew the difference between healthy education and miseducation.

Intellectually gifted children present another, different example of the structural imperative. First of all, intellectual giftedness and creative talent are not the same; in fact, they represent two different modes of thought. Intellectual giftedness reflects what has been called "convergent thinking," thinking that moves along conventional lines. Talented youngsters, in contrast, tend to think in "divergent" ways which deviate from conventional modes of thought. Talented children such as Dalit are creative and original, while intellectually gifted children are mentally precocious.[14]

What is often striking about intellectually gifted youngsters is how much they have acquired of conventional knowledge. Such children read early and quickly master bodies of knowledge of the conventional sort: math, history, science, and so on. In the case of intellectually gifted youngsters, the structural imperative takes the form of accelerated learning and mastery of conventional forms of knowledge:

> Kevin Kaliher is 10. He has an IQ of 169. His least favorite question, he says, is "How did you get so smart?" His answer, "I guess I was born that way."
> Kevin has scored almost 700 (of a possible 800) on the math portion of the SAT. . . . He is now in the ninth grade at Lake Forest Academy in Lake Forest, Ill. Still he insists in a voice that is quiet but assured, "I'm really a normal kid—just a little smart." Kevin amuses himself by working with graphics on his Franklin Ace 1000 home computer and by studying piano and violin.[15]

It might seem that intellectually gifted children are the exception to the rule about the negatives of formal instruction at an early age. After all, these children are doing at the age of five or six what most children are doing at the age of twelve or thirteen. Wouldn't such children profit from early formal instruction, since they are ready for it? Not really. In fact, what intellectually talented youngsters need most is a prolongation of the kind of educational program I have suggested is appropriate to five- and six-year-olds.

What has to be remembered is that intellectually talented youngsters have the structural imperative in the extreme! For most children, the structural imperative dissipates once the structures are fully formed (around the age of seven for concrete operations), at which time more traditional motivations such as attachments, self-esteem, and competitiveness come into play. But for intellectually gifted children the structural imperative does not dissipate, perhaps because such youngsters are already moving into the next stage of structural imperative, which does not appear in most young people until the age of twelve or thirteen—the higher-order mental abilities which Piaget called formal operations.

What intellectually gifted children need most, then, is not early formal instruction but rather a prolongation of opportunities to explore and investigate on their own. The task of the teacher of such children is not to instruct in the conventional sense but to do what the early-childhood educator does, only at a higher level. Much more critical than direct instruction for the realization of their intellectual potential is the providing of the right science material, the right literature, the right math materials, along with thoughtful guidance on what directions to take.

That schools do not often provide for the gifted or talented individual's structural imperative is clear from the biographies of famous persons:

> Thomas Edison said of school, "I remember that I was never able to get along at school. I was always at the foot of the class. I used to feel the teachers did not sympathize with me and that my father thought I was stupid." . . .
>
> Albert Einstein was considered dull by his teachers and by his parents. His son Albert Jr. said, "Actually, I understand my father was a very well behaved child. He was shy, lonely and withdrawn from the world even then. He was even considered backward by his teachers. He told me that his teachers reported to his father, that he was mentally slow, unsociable and adrift forever in his foolish dreams.[16]

In their classic study of five hundred persons of eminence, the Goertzels found that more than three hundred of these people had had serious school problems:

Their dissatisfactions were: with the curriculum; with dull, irrational or cruel teachers; with other students who bullied, ignored or bored them, and with school failure. In general it was the totality of the school situation with which they were concerned, and they seldom have one clear-cut isolated complaint. [17]

For the gifted and talented, then, formal instruction is miseducation at all age levels! Fortunately, for many of these individuals the structural imperative is powerful enough to enable them to find on their own the nourishment they need to realize their abilities. But this is not the case for the average child. For children of five or six, even free play might be more beneficial than formal instruction. Such instruction may inhibit children's realization of their abilities and give rise to a sense of helplessness that is more dominant than their sense of competence.

CHILD'S PLAY

While play is important at all levels of development, it takes on particular significance in the sixth and seventh years of life (when children are five and six) when the balance of competence and helplessness is determined. During this critical period, the child's budding sense of competence is frequently under attack, not only from inappropriate instructional practices that hinder the structural imperative, but also from the hundred and one feelings of hurt, frustration, and rejection that mark a child's entrance into the world of schooling, competition, and peer-group involvement. Again and again the young child's sense of competence in his or her abilities may be challenged by adults and by age mates.

Young children, however, have none of the adult ego defenses (such as rationalization, reaction formation, and projection) which we attain when we are older and with which we defend ourselves against attacks upon our competence and self-esteem. That is why play is so important: it is young children's only defense against the many real or imagined attacks and slights they encounter. In play, children can assert their competence as "superheroes" more powerful and competent than the most powerful and competent adult. Through dramatic play and role-playing, they can assert their competence to assume adult roles eventually. And through their play with peers they assert their social competence, their ability to make and keep friends. Play is always a transformation of reality in the service of the self.

This function of play in early childhood, as a means of reasserting the child's sense of competence, is often misunderstood. It is either rationalized as the "child's work," by which is meant another way in which children learn reading, writing, and science. Or it is explained as the avenue through which children express their creative powers, with the suggestion that they need some formal instruction in expressing themselves more adequately. To be sure, young children do learn something from their play, and it does reflect some of their creative potentials, but neither of these is its prime function.

The misunderstanding regarding the function of play for young children often results in miseducation. If play is thought of as the child's "work," then it may be translated into a lesson plan. A child playing store may be asked to put prices on his wares and total up the sales. And if play is thought of as the expression of the child's creative impulse, she may be asked to say what her drawing or painting is and to make the sky and grass more conventional colors. Unfortunately, such treatments of the child's play do not encourage the sense of competence, but rather the reverse: they contribute to a sense of helplessness.

I think we all have memories of experiences like the following which can have a powerful, lifelong impact. As a kindergarten child I loved to sing, my way of playing and asserting my competence although I could not carry a tune. When a dignitary came to visit, our teacher had the class sing for this person. But before she began to lead the children in song, the teacher pointed at me and said, "You, Elkind, you are a listener." It was not only my career as a singer that was ended in kindergarten; so, too, was my career as an artist. After I had finished a magnificent collage on a large red piece of construction paper, I had a brilliant idea. I took my scissors and rounded the corners. When the teacher looked at it, she said, "You have ruined it." I must say that I did have a poem published in the school paper when I was nine, and that determined my career as a writer.

The point is that we have to respect children's play productions as their efforts to protect, defend, and enhance their sense of competence. With such productions, the old adage "If you can't say anything good, then don't say anything at all" is the rule to follow. If we make ample provisions for children to engage in a variety of play activities without making them into something they are not or evaluating the children's productions, we contribute to their sense of competence. Otherwise, we rob the children of their major defense against the feeling of helplessness.

The fifth and sixth years of life, then, are critical for the attainment of a sense of industry and a sense of competence. Once children enter school, we are no longer primarily responsible for the balance of those children's personality potentials; schools have responsibility, too. Schooling practices become as important as parenting practices in the outcome of the crises of personality potentials. Just as we know what parenting practices encourage and support trust, autonomy, initiative, and belonging, so do we know what schooling practices encourage industry and competence.

When we recognize the young child's unique modes of learning and adapt educational practices to them, we engage in healthy education. When we ignore what we know about how young children learn, and expose them to teaching practices appropriate to children at older age levels, we miseducate them and put them at risk for a sense of inferiority and helplessness. We need to overcome our wrong ideas about superkids and child competence, and to provide young children with the experiences that will allow them to emerge from kindergarten and first grade with a robust sense of industry and competence, and an eagerness and enthusiasm for further schooling.

HEALTHY
EDUCATION

8

Making Healthy
Educational Choices

WHEN OUR CHILDREN are young we must make several important educational decisions. If we have the choice, should we or should we not enroll our young child in an early-education program? If we decide we do want our child in such a program, or if our careers or financial situation demand that we put our child in an early-childhood program, which program should it be? And then comes the next and sometimes difficult set of decisions: when and where to enroll our child in kindergarten? We can make these decisions in a more informed way if we can identify healthy early-childhood education and if we know all our options regarding kindergarten enrollment.

To Enroll or Not Enroll

Some of us are fortunate in being able to choose whether or not to enroll our child in one or another preschool program. And the range of choices is enormous, everything from "Gymboree" to a full-day "academic" preschool. As I have suggested in earlier chapters, some of these programs put children at risk for no purpose and should be eliminated from consideration; others, such as Gymboree, may be fun for the child and a socializing opportunity for parents and thus pose no problem.

For some parents, the real issue is whether or not to enroll a child in a nursery school program. In general, if it is a true early-childhood program, it can benefit both you and your child. It enlivens social experience by giving your child an opportunity to be with other adults and with a group of children of the same age. Because the range of toys and equipment is much greater than can be provided at home, the nursery school offers additional opportunities for the child to enhance a sense of autonomy, initiative, and competence. And a teacher trained in early-childhood education can provide the individual and group guidance and direction children require to get the most out of their activities.

On the other hand, nursery school is not essential for healthy development. If you have the time and energy to provide your child with a variety of social and educational experiences, you can also provide a rich early-childhood program for your child at home. To do this, you need to learn some of the basic principles of early-childhood education (e.g., the importance of putting concrete experience before any label for experience), provide your child with appropriate manipulative learning materials, and guide him or her in using these materials in the most productive way. Other children in the neighborhood can occasionally be brought together in play groups to round out your child's early-childhood education program.

Does this mean that early-childhood education in the form of nursery school is of no value? Not at all. The situation is analogous to home schooling at later age levels. Some parents have decided that they have the time, energy, and commitment to educate their children at home and often do quite a good job of it. But schools are still necessary for all those parents who do not choose, for whatever reason, to educate their children at home. The same holds true for nursery school. It is important for all those children whose parents decide, for whatever reason, that they cannot provide the intellectual, social, and emotional enrichment provided by the nursery school.

IDENTIFYING HEALTHY EARLY-CHILDHOOD PROGRAMS

Miseducation is always makeshift, jerry-rigged to satisfy the social dynamics of a particular historical moment. Healthy early-childhood education, in contrast, has a long and distinguished history. The unique character of early-childhood education has been asserted by the authorities of educational theory: Jean Jacques Rousseau, Johann Pestalozzi, Friedrich Froebel, Maria Montessori, Rudolf Steiner, and John Dewey. And their theories have been elaborated, refined, and honed by successive generations of practitioners. Healthy early-childhood education today is a model of what education at all age levels should be: the evolutionary product of continuous growth and development rather than the superficial glitz of still another educational fad.

Today healthy early-education programs can be found in home-care settings, in public and private nursery schools, in public and private day-care centers, and in public as well as private pre-kindergartens, kindergartens, and even, in some cases, first grades. Regardless of the setting, what all healthy education programs have in common is their suitability for young children. Such programs recognize the very special character of young children—their size, their learning modes, their many strengths, their special limitations. That is the lesson which all the authorities on early-childhood education taught in their own special ways and in their own special language.

Healthy Early-Childhood Education: What to Look For

Given the diversity of early-childhood programs, how can we tell which ones provide healthy education and which ones miseducate? I have been working in nursery schools and kindergartens for more than a quarter of a century and have learned to tell pretty quickly which programs provide healthy early-childhood education and which miseducate. So I would like you now to join me as I walk through various early-education programs and point out the sorts of furnishings, materials, and practices a parent should be alert to.

The first thing one needs to do in evaluating early-education programs is to listen with your eyes and not with your ears. The educational philosophy espoused by the director of an early-childhood facility may have nothing at all to do with what goes on in the school! I once visited a nursery school in a low-income Los Angeles suburb. The school was in a small bungalow with a postage-stamp backyard. I was impressed by the bustle of activity. Inside, one group of children was cooking, another was making zithers, while still another was painting still lifes from a most artistically arranged bowl of fruit. In the yard were a small boat and the fuselage of a small airplane. Children waited eagerly to take their turn steering the boat or flying the plane.

When I asked the woman who ran the school how she arrived at this extraordinary setting, she really surprised me. She began telling me that she was a student of Skinner, of learning theory and behavior modification! The entire school, she continued, was built upon strict learning-theory principles. I am sure that she believed what she said and really didn't see the discrepancy between her philosophy and her practice. And it is a most important point to remember in evaluating any early-childhood setting.

In general, I have found that regardless of the label—Montessori, Waldorf, Play, Behavioral, or what not—teachers who know young children are much more alike in practice than those who do not. That is to say, you can find two Montessori schools that are much further apart in practice than a Montessori school and a traditional nursery school. The same, by the way, is true of therapists for children. Good therapists, regardless of whether they are Freudian, Jungian, Skinnerian, Rankian, and so on, are quite alike in their actual practice with children. In a word, when evaluating an early-childhood program don't go by the label!

It does not harm to ask whether the director and staff have degrees in early-childhood education. While such training may not be essential to healthy early-childhood teaching (some teachers can pick up the necessary training on the job), it is an added assurance that the school is based on a solid early-childhood foundation. It is also important to ask about the teacher-to-child ratio. A useful rule of thumb is that the number of children per adult should be no more than three times the child's age. That is to say, for one-year-olds no more than three to one; for two-year-olds, no more than six to one, and so on. These ratios are ideal, of course, but a healthy class should not go too far beyond them. For children of five and below, class sizes of more than twenty children to an adult do not easily accommodate healthy education.

Let us imagine now that we are walking into a nursery school or day-care center. To orient myself, the first thing I look for is a block corner. A good set of large wooden blocks, even if these are sanded pieces of two-by-four, is the first indication of a healthy educational program. Blocks are a fundamental learning material for young children. Two- and three-year-olds can climb up on them and use them for large and small motor control. Four- and five-year-olds can build with them and incorporate them into a variety of play and social activities. Block work or play can thus help develop children's sense of autonomy and initiative, as well as their sense of industry, competence, and belonging.

Next, I look for plants and animals. A hamster, a few gerbils, or a rabbit are usual. Animals provide important learning experiences for young children. Not only do the children learn to identify them, but they also learn about feeding them and cleaning their cages—the child's first experience of taking care of someone else. Young children may also get their first exposure to reproduction if the animals breed. Plants are equally important. Like animals, plants give children experience with caring for living things that are dependent upon them. Plants provide new colors and forms for children to learn and an opportunity to observe the growth of living things. Taking care of plants and animals is of particular important for the child's sense of competence.

I also look for a reading area, either a bookcase or book rack with a variety of children's books. There should be picture books in abundance, well-illustrated books of fairy tales, rhymes, and poetry. Contemporary writers such as Dr. Seuss and Ezra Jack Keats should be represented. It pleases me when I see a piece of carpet and pillows for children to lie on while looking at the books or when there is a child-sized rocker or two for children to sit on while they turn the pages. In some schools the reading area is combined with a record player or tape recorder so the space can double as a music area as well. Such reading corners support and encourage the child's sense of initiative.

Another area to look for is dramatic play. Somewhere in the room one should find some abandoned adult clothing, particularly discarded men's and women's hats, shoes, and shirts, which children can put on when they are playing "store," "house," "fire station," and so on. There should also be a couple of easels for painting and one or two large tables, or several small ones, where children can work with clay, color, finger-paint, make collages, and even practice making letters.

I also look to see if there is a carpentry area with a table where children can pound nails and, under supervision, saw small pieces of wood. A science corner with materials for weighing, measuring, and magnifying and a water table for play and experimentation are also very desirable. A special plus is a piano or a guitar and a teacher who knows how to play them. But there should be instruments children can play—a triangle, a set of bells or cymbals, or a xylophone.

The arrangement of the classroom into "interest areas" is particularly supportive of the child's sense of initiative inasmuch as it provides opportunities for the child to choose the area he or she would like to work in. Nor does the arrangement into interest areas contradict what I said about the permeability of the young child's learning: these are "interest," not subject-matter, areas and the child can and does learn many different kinds of concepts in each area.

So far we have looked at the various parts of the inside area, but we need to look at it as a whole as well. The room should not be too cluttered, and the traffic-flow patterns for the children—from one activity to another—should be easy to navigate. I also notice whether the room seems to be cleaned regularly and whether the materials are well looked after and in good supply. I am more impressed with a school offering less material that is well looked after than with a school where the material is abundant but looks shoddy.

Next, we need to proceed to the outdoor areas. Ideally, the play area should be directly accessible from the classroom, since this arrangement is often safer and saves time. A good play area should have a large, safe climbing apparatus. The front seat of an old boat, car, or the like, appropriately smoothed, painted, and safety-proofed, provides an outdoor setting for dramatic play. Swings, slides, a large sandbox, and a paved track for tricycles are other things to look for in the outdoor area. Again, the equipment should be well looked after and in good repair. The play area should also be fully enclosed.

So far, we have looked at the static aspects of a healthy early-childhood program; now we need to consider how children actually live in this environment. A typical morning might go something like this. After the children arrive and get their street clothes off (and into individual "cubbies" appropriately labeled with their names and pictures), they often come together in a circle to talk about the morning's activities. The children may take the roll, name the day of the week, note the date and the temperature. If a particular child is having a birthday, this is duly noted, and usually the child's mother has sent cookies or cupcakes for the children to have in addition to their snacks to celebrate the day.

Although it is less common than it once was, I still feel that the "Show and Tell" portion of the beginning circle meeting is an important one. During this portion of the group activity, each child may tell about some important life event that has occurred since the group last met: the birth of a sibling, the acquisition of a new pet, a special trip, the visit of a relative, are all worthy of note. Sometimes children are able to bring something to illustrate the event. One child, for example, showed a piece of sugarcane her father had brought back from Hawaii. Show and Tell is particularly helpful in enhancing a child's sense of belonging.

After the Show and Tell, children will often disperse to different interest areas. Some will migrate to the block corner, others to the dramatic play area, still others to the reading center. A skilled teacher makes sure that children have a variety of experiences and do not spend their time exclusively in one area. The teacher will work with individual children or with a small group of children on a special project such as making a collage, measuring things like hands or feet, or baking cookies. Toward the middle of the morning, all the children come together for a snack, usually juice and crackers.

It is in the small-group activities that the skill of an early-childhood educator is most in evidence. Effective early-childhood education always involves knowing how to avoid either over- or understructuring an activity. When working at the water table, for example, the teacher might ask the children whether the cork or the key will float, and why? The teacher has structured the activity by selecting the materials for the demonstration but will follow the children's lead when it comes to the direction the discussion should take. A child who says the cork floats "because it is round" might be asked to find other round things and try them out.

Choosing the right materials is as important as being able to follow up on the direction of a child's thinking. In one school I visited, the teacher was working with a small group of children around a large food scale on which she was placing pinecones. She was asking children whether four pinecones weighed more than two. But a scale of that sort is inappropriate for young children, since they still have no unit concepts and don't know what the numbers on the scale mean. And the weight of pinecones is not intuitively obvious. The teacher's purpose would have been better served with a balance scale and a feather and a nail.

After the individual and small-group activity, the children may engage in one or another large-group activity. Sometimes the teacher will read a story to the children; sometimes they will sing songs or play a group game such as "Simon Says." After this group activity, children will usually go outdoors to the play area. Out of doors, children choose the play activity they wish to engage in. After the outside play, children usually come back for a quiet activity and begin preparing to be picked up and to go home if it is a nursery school, or for lunch if it is a full-day nursery school, kindergarten, or day-care program.

If it is a full-day program, the afternoon is generally less active than the morning. Most children, like most adults, learn best in the morning, and that is the time for the most demanding intellectual tasks. Moreover, the energy reserves of young children are usually run down by early afternoon, and many preschool youngsters are ready for a nap after a full morning of activity. Full-day programs should have portable cots or mats for children to rest on. For children who do not wish or do not need to nap, listening to records, looking at books, or being read to are all quiet activities. When all of the children are up, group games are another activity to fill the early afternoon hours. This is also the time when children might be allowed to watch television programs such as "Mr. Rogers' Neighborhood."

In describing a typical day, I have left out several activities which may not be done on a daily basis but which are very important. Taking children for walks and outings is a very important learning experience. Children may walk to the local fire station or to a bakery or restaurant that will allow them to visit "behind the scenes," so to speak. The school may also have special "visitors," such as adults who come to perform for them. Other guests may engage children in singing, rhythmic movement activities, and so on. These activities, and a panorama of changing projects from making masks at Halloween to painting eggs for Easter, provide continual variety and interest for young children.

Obviously, not all early-childhood settings will have all of the features that I have described. Montessori schools, for example, are usually rich in materials such as blocks, form boards, beads for number learning, and pictures for concept learning. Yet these schools may have little in the way of dramatic play materials, sandboxes, and the like. This need not be a problem if children have adequate play time and materials at home. More important is that the Montessori materials are age-appropriate ones that children find stimulating and that capture their intellectual attention for extended periods of time.

Although I have focused upon healthy educational programs, it is also necessary to say what I may see that tells me that the program is not age-appropriate. If I see workbooks with little problems for children to fill in the "right" answer, this is a very bad sign. Workbooks have no place in healthy early-childhood education. Certainly, young children can begin to practice making letters and numbers and solving problems, but this should be done without workbooks. Young children need to learn initiative, autonomy, industry, and competence before they learn that answers can be right or wrong.

Another practice to watch out for is group drill. The danger here is that the young child might get fixated on rote learning, the modus operandi of group drill. Early childhood is the time when children establish their learning styles, and if not encouraged to utilize a variety of styles (which the interest areas do), the child can become fixated on a particular learning style that can be of disadvantage to him or her later. For example, when I was running a small school, I had one eight-year-old who had been taught since kindergarten by means of group drill. He approached every task as if it were an exercise in rote learning. It took us a year of hard work to get him to utilize other learning styles.

These, then, are some of the things to look for in choosing a healthy educational program for your child. No program is ideal in the sense of exactly fitting the above description, as well as being convenient and also inexpensive. Compromises are always necessary. Enrolling a child in a program with less than the full complement of healthy early-childhood education ingredients will still benefit the child and buffer the stress of separation from parents. On the other hand, putting a young child in a high-pressure academic program is not a compromise, it is a surrender to social pressure, or to personal anxiety, or to both. What should not be compromised is the idea of healthy education.

KINDERGARTEN ENTRANCE AND THE AGE EFFECT

A child's kindergarten and first-grade experiences are critical in the determination of whether that child's sense of industry and of competence will be stronger than his or her sense of inferiority and helplessness. And how these psychosocial crises are resolved will have significant consequences for the young person's long-term academic and vocational success. It is of the greatest importance, then, to ensure that the child has positive and successful experiences in kindergarten and first grade.

It is simply a truism in schooling that the youngest children in kindergarten and first-grade classes do more poorly than do the oldest children in these classes. As we shall see, it really does not make any difference whether the youngest children in a kindergarten are four years old and the oldest five years old, or whether the youngest children in the kindergarten are five and the oldest six. What happens is that the curriculum seems always to be geared to the oldest rather than to the youngest children. As the age of the oldest children in the kindergarten goes up, so, too, do the demands of the curriculum.

Schools have tried to cope with this "age effect" in a number of different ways. More than a quarter of a century ago, some school systems adopted an A and B system. Children with winter and spring birthdays entered school in January, so that their school year ended in December. Children with summer and fall birthdays entered kindergarten in the fall, so that their school year ended in June. But the system became too cumbersome and was abandoned. After looking at some of the programmatic ways in which contemporary schools are attempting to cope with the age effect, we can look at some of our options as parents.

SCHOOLS AND THE AGE EFFECT

Schools have attempted to deal with the age effect by changing the entrance age for kindergarten, by introducing "transition" classes, and by mandating across-the-board "readiness" testing or screening for all children who are about to enter kindergarten or first grade.

Age of Entrance

Over the last thirty years, schools have been raising the age at which children are permitted to enter kindergarten. According to the Educational Research Service, most states in 1958 required that children be five by December or January if they were to be admitted the preceding fall. In 1985 some 80 percent of the states did not permit a child to enter kindergarten in September who had been born after November 1 of that same fall. In some school districts in Missouri, Colorado, and elsewhere, the entrance age is being cut back still further into the summer months.

There are many reasons for this elevation of the entrance age. For one thing, publicly supported kindergarten has now become part of public education in all of the states, although it is still not mandatory in many communities. With more children entering kindergarten, the limitations of the younger children become more pronounced as their number increases. Raising the entrance age serves to keep the younger and less prepared children out of kindergarten.

Unfortunately, raising the age for kindergarten entrance does not always have the desired effect. As kindergarten has become commonplace, first-grade teachers have changed their academic expectations for the children entering their classrooms. When only some of the children entering first grade had attended kindergarten, it was unreasonable to expect that all children entering first grade would know letter sounds, be able to count to ten, and be able to cooperate with other children. Accordingly, the first-grade teacher of the past was more prepared to be flexible with respect to the range of academic and social skills the children brought with them.

Now that kindergarten has become all but universal, the expectations of first-grade teachers have become more uniform. Since all children entering first grade have been to kindergarten, they should know letter sounds, counting, and cooperation. Now a child who enters first grade without these academic or social skills is regarded as deficient. These new demands upon children entering first grade have changed the character of kindergarten education. Now kindergarten teachers feel they must prepare children for first grade. This, in turn, has pushed kindergarten teachers into doing more formal instruction than they had done in the past.

The transformation of kindergarten into a recognized part of public education rather than a kind of nursery school has had the effect of changing parental expectations as well. If a child does not bring home work papers, some parents feel that the child is not learning anything and the school is not doing its job. Like first-grade teachers, parents now expect children, by the time they leave kindergarten, to have achieved certain academic goals that will have prepared them for first grade.

In effect, we now have a new concept of the "academic" kindergarten which, no less than the new concept of the competent child, has been determined more by social and economic considerations than by what we know is good pedagogy for children. As I have already pointed out, the cross-cultural data is clear in demonstrating that a later introduction to formal schooling is more beneficial than an earlier one. By making the kindergarten more "academic," we are ensuring that a significant proportion of kindergarten children will experience miseducation and have their sense of industry and competence put at risk.

Raising the entrance age for kindergarten entrance has thus not had the desired effect. What is gained by denying younger children entrance to kindergarten is lost by raising the academic demands upon the older children who are admitted.

Transition Classes

Another programmatic strategy for dealing with the mismatch between children and first-grade curricula is what has come to be called "transition" or "pre-first-grade" classes. Such classes were instituted to avoid the stigma of a child's "repeating" kindergarten while at the same time moving the child a step nearer to being ready for the first grade. Children, however, are not fooled by this way of disguising their having "flunked" kindergarten. Nonetheless, a majority of parents, teachers, and administrators subscribe to the belief that having a child repeat kindergarten will remedy any maturity difficulties the child might have in accommodating to the demands of schooling.

Unfortunately, the available research on the effectiveness of transition classes does not support the benefits of such "gifts of time."[1] In reviewing five studies that looked at the effects of transition classes on school achievement, Gredeler[2] found that in only one of the investigations did the children in the transition class show a significantly higher academic achievement than did socially promoted children (children who did not attend transition classes but went directly into first grade). Other studies have also shown that children who were retained because they were not ready or mature enough for first grade did no better than children who had been given the same evaluation but who had not been held back.[3]

After their review of the research on transition classes, Shephard and Smith conclude:

> Despite the promises, providing an extra year before first grade does not solve the problem it was intended to solve. Children in these programs show virtually no advantage over equally at-risk children who have not had the extra year. Furthermore, there is often an emotional cost associated with staying back, even when parents and teachers are very enlightened about presenting the decision to the child.[4]

Testing

Can the potential damage of being the youngest in the class be avoided by testing? Is it possible to identify those children who will or will not succeed in kindergarten by means of one or another kind of test? Many school systems believe that this is indeed the case and are employing a bewildering variety of tests to assess children's readiness for school, to measure their achievement, and to screen children with potential learning problems. A survey of 177 school districts in New York State in 1977 found that some 151 different tests and procedures were being used for screening. In a 1984 survey in Michigan, 111 different tests were being used to evaluate children in preschool, kindergarten, and first grade.

Readiness tests are essentially measures of general ability and are comparable to intelligence tests. The Gesell (readiness) tests, for example, are designed to assess the child's social, emotional, motor, and intellectual maturity relative to other children. With such tests, any given child's performance is compared with the performance of a large group of children of the same age. Children who score below the norm for their age group would be considered "young" for their age and perhaps not ready for school. Unfortunately, Readiness tests also correlate with intelligence tests: this means that a child who scores low on Readiness could be either immature or low in mental ability.

Readiness tests are not good predictors of the child's academic performance at the early grades. This has partly to do with the tests and partly to do with the conditions of schooling. Young children are not good test takers, and unless the examiner is very experienced and proficient the chances of getting an inaccurate reading of the child's ability are about as great as those of getting an accurate one. And the test does not say how the child will fare when placed with children of greater or less maturity, which is what happens in the schools.

Achievement tests attempt to assess children's proficiency in very specific domains, such as reading and math. The widely used Metropolitan Achievement Tests are a case in point. Although these tests are called "achievement" they really establish the child's current skill level with respect to reading and math. They are thus useful to teachers who wish to match instruction to the child's level of proficiency. Whether teachers actually have the freedom, time, and energy to individualize in the way suggested by the tests is quite another matter.

Screening tests are used to identify children who might need special education services. Such tests are comparable to the tests for vision and hearing that are routinely given to children to detect any visual or hearing defect that might impair the child's learning. Tests like the McCarthy screening test aim to identify children who have potential learning problems and who might need remedial work. While such tests can be useful in the hands of a well-trained, experienced examiner, they can often give as many false as positive signs of potential learning problems.

Although a wide proliferation of tests is being used in schools all over the country to assess readiness, achievement, and potential learning problems, none of these are without their limitations. Testing is costly and time-consuming, yet the overall results often do not seem to warrant the investment. The basic error in testing for readiness is that it locates the problem in the children rather than where it has to be placed, namely, in the match between the child and the school program.

PARENT OPTIONS FOR DEALING WITH THE AGE EFFECT

As parents, we have several options additional to those provided by the schools for dealing with the age effect. One of these is to retain our children at home if we feel they are not ready to meet the demands of schooling. Another option is to send our children to a private kindergarten and first grade that has a curriculum sufficiently flexible to accommodate the diversity of maturity levels young children bring with them to school.

Delaying Entry

One of the most difficult questions parents of children with summer or fall birthdays have to make is whether to enroll their child in kindergarten that fall, with the result that the child will be one of the youngest in the class, or wait a year, with the result that the child will be one of the oldest. Delaying a child's entrance into kindergarten is quite different from having the child held back once in school. Once a child is in school, the negative effects of school failure cannot be undone by repeating or by moving the child into a transition class.

Delaying school entry, however, is quite another matter. A child whose entrance into kindergarten has been delayed has not experienced school failure during the year spent at home or in an out-of-home setting. The research is quite consistent in showing that children who are among the oldest in their kindergarten class do better academically and socially than those who are among the youngest in the class.[5]

A study carried out in Grosse Pointe, Michigan, is instructive. After a fourteen-year longitudinal study, the Grosse Pointe schools abandoned an early entrance program for very bright children. The reasons for abandoning the program were:

1. Nearly one-third of early entrants turned out to be poorly adjusted.

2. Only one-twentieth of early entrants were judged to be outstanding leaders at the end of the experiment.

3. Nearly three out of four were considered entirely lacking in leadership.

4. Approximately one in four of the very bright early school entrants either was below average in school or had to repeat a grade.[6]

It is important to emphasize that the effects of entrance age are relative rather than absolute. A Hawaiian study makes this point very well. In Hawaii, the cut-off date for school entrance is December 31. Examination of the school records of 154,000 pupils in the Hawaii schools showed that December-born children were twice as likely as January-born children to have been diagnosed as learning-disabled.[7]

Nor do the effects of being the youngest in the class disappear with age. A study in Wapakoneta, Ohio, compared children with summer birthdays who had and had not entered school just after turning five. All the pupils in the study had completed third grade, and some had completed sixth grade. The results were impressive. Among the boys who had delayed entrance, 79 percent had above-average grades compared to only 27 percent of those who had entered early. For the girls, 71 percent of the late entrants had above-average scores compared to only 22 percent for the early entrants.[8]

The conclusion could hardly be less escapable: a child who is one of the oldest in a kindergarten class is much more likely to do well academically than a child who is among the youngest in the class! There is a strong incentive, then, to delay entrance for a child with a summer or fall birthday. Unfortunately, delayed entrance may not be a viable option for some parents who cannot afford to keep their child out of school for an extra year.

Private Schools

There is another option that some parents can exercise if they are not really happy with what is provided by the public schools. Programs such as Montessori and the Waldorf Schools and many private schools offer small classes, individualized instruction, and flexible, child-centered curricula which can accommodate to the child and do not demand that the child do all of the accommodating.

Montessori Schools. The Montessori schools are derived from the work of the famed Italian physician and educator Maria Montessori. Montessori was very much aware of the unique modes of learning in young children and designed a wide range of materials nicely suited to the manipulative, permeable nature of young children's learning. Her materials are also self-didactic (in putting a puzzle together, children can see their own mistakes), which allows children to direct and take responsibility for their own learning. It was also Montessori who introduced child-sized chairs and tables to early-childhood education.

Montessori schools have the reputation of being academic. While this is true, it is true in a healthy sense. Children are exposed to reading and writing at the preschool level, but in very concrete ways. Children learn, for example, to discriminate sandpaper letters and to do their own writing by assembling letters made of wood. Children learn sight function words (e.g., "Stop," "Go") and the words for shapes and colors only after these have been learned. Although there is considerable variation among Montessori schools, the teachers are uniformly well trained, the curriculum is flexible and child-centered, and children are allowed to move along at their own pace. Many Montessori schools now go up to the primary grades, and some go as high as high school.

Waldorf Schools. The Waldorf schools are derived from the writings and practice of the German philosopher and educator Rudolf Steiner. Steiner was troubled by the overly academic emphasis of schools; he felt that the aesthetic side of children was being overlooked and that this should be developed along with the intellectual powers. The Waldorf schools emphasize creativity in all aspects of children's work. Teachers and children create their own curricula and books. The same teacher may stay with the same group of children for as many as eight grades. In so doing, the teacher has to grow and learn with the children, a very positive example of what good teaching and learning should be.

Other Private Schools. Many private schools provide small, unpressured classes where children can move into academics at their own pace. In some of these schools there is "multi-age" grouping, where the same teacher has both kindergarten and first-grade children. This arrangement has many advantages. For one thing, a kindergarten teacher who really knows a child by the end of the year must then pass on the child to the first-grade teacher, who has to start from scratch. With the same child for two years, the teacher can really follow through with what the child has learned. Second, because there is such a wide range of ability, there will always be a small ability group for the child to fit into. Finally, since the children who are the youngest the first year are the oldest children the second year, they will experience the positive benefits of being older.

Before sending your child to a private school, shop around. Visit a Montessori school, a Waldorf school, and some other private schools. Ask about the program and visit the classrooms. A good kindergarten classroom should have many of the features of a healthy educational program I described earlier. When talking to the kindergarten teacher, ask about his or her general goals and what the teacher expects the children to accomplish by the end of the year. If the teacher has half a dozen general goals (e.g., expects that the children will know letter sounds and numbers), this is preferable to a teacher who has a great many precise goals (e.g., expects the child to know fifty sight words, five colors, four geometric forms). The former teacher is putting the child before the curriculum, while the latter teacher is doing the reverse.

Conclusion

Parents who have a child with a summer or fall birthday and who can afford to keep their child home for a year or to put the child in a private school clearly have an advantage over parents who have a child with a summer or fall birthday but who are financially less fortunate. This is a very inequitable situation brought about by the failure of the schools to address the problem of the age effect adequately.

The solution cannot reside in policy changes such as raising the entrance age, the provision of "transition" classes, or mandatory "readiness" testing or "screening." None of these policy manipulations speaks to the real issue, which is the inflexible, academically demanding curricula now prevailing in our kindergartens. An equitable solution has to come from the schools, not from parents and children.

Schools can eliminate the handicap experienced by the youngest children in the kindergarten group by changing the curricula in the kindergarten and the first grade so that they resemble early-childhood classrooms rather than second- and third-grade classrooms. This "liberation" of the kindergarten and first grade from their domination by elementary education should also be accompanied by the elimination of grades and workbooks and by providing teachers trained in early-childhood education. In the long run, this "liberation" of the kindergarten and first grade will do more than any of the makeshift remedies currently being employed to eliminate the widespread miseducation of young children in our schools.

9

Questions Parents Ask

IN THIS CHAPTER I would like to give myself a second chance. For the last several years I have been lecturing extensively in all parts of this country and Canada. I speak to parents, to educators, and to health professionals. In my lectures I cover, in a condensed fashion, much of the material that is in this book. After my lectures, if time and circumstances permit, I entertain questions. Often, long after the question-and-answer period is over, I think about my answers and wish I had answered differently or more completely. In this chapter I would like to answer again some of the questions I have been asked, but this time with the benefit of time for reflection.

Q. You say that young children should not be taught to read and do math, but what about the child who asks you to teach her to read? My daughter kept asking me the names and sounds of the letters, and how to say words she saw printed, and before I knew it, she was reading—she taught herself! Should I not have given her the names and sounds, should I not have told what the words said?

A. I think you did exactly the right thing. No roadblocks of any kind should be put in the way of children who want to read on their own, and we should support and encourage children in their eagerness to begin reading. You can never miseducate children by responding appropriately to their demands for information.

But your child is the exception, for only 1 to 3 percent of children are reading with comprehension before they enter kindergarten. The majority of children do not show interest in the mechanics of reading until after the age of five or six, and we do miseducate them if we introduce such mechanics before children show any inclination in that direction.

Q. What about discipline? In talking about trust, autonomy, industry, and the like you don't say anything about discipline. You make it sound as if children never misbehave and that all we have to do is support and encourage. But we support and encourage our daughter and she still defies us and gives us a hard time. What do you do when support and encouragement don't work? Can you give me some techniques I can use when she refuses to go to bed, or to put away her things?

A. Discipline is an attitude, not a technique. When we as parents feel that we are in charge of the situation, we communicate this sense of being in charge to our child. If, on the other hand, we feel unsure of our ability to control our child's behavior, we will communicate that as well. One of the values of knowing about child development, about how children think and feel and what psychosocial stage they are at, is that it gives us a greater sense of mastery over the situation.

But knowledge is really not enough; our own sense of competence is at issue. That is why rearing later-born children is always easier than raising firstborns. We are so much more experienced and proficient the second time around, so much more confident in our ability to handle a variety of situations, that we communicate this sense of competence to our children. It does not eliminate the need to exercise our authority, but it makes the exercise of that authority easier.

In my lectures, when no one is willing to ask the first question, I say, "I will now take the second question." For many of us it would be easier if we could start with the second child!

In general, though, what is crucial to discipline is your mind-set. When I see children who dominate their parents, it is always because the parents really feel they have no control. What you need to tell yourself is that you are the adult and the child is the child. You are the one in charge and in control, not the child. And children do not want to be in charge or in control. They will take over if you let them, but it is frightening for them as well as for you. The best discipline is to say what you mean and mean what you say.

Q. You paint a pretty grim picture of miseducation. But are we really doing such bad things to our children? Okay, so we dress them up in designer clothes, send them to the gym, and have them take music lessons. So what is so terrible? What about the parents who abandon, abuse, neglect, and reject their children? We who are doing so much for our kids are the "good" guys, and what I can't understand is why you are after us and not the "bad" guys.

A. It is because you are the good guys that I am troubled. When immature, self-centered, and cruel people do harm to their children, it is criminal. But when loving, caring, well-intentioned parents put their children at risk for no purpose, it is tragic. Of course there is nothing wrong with dressing a child in designer clothes, with taking a child to the gym or providing music lessons. But it is also a fact of life that good things misused can turn into bad things. It is only when we provide luxuries and lessons for children at too early an age and for the wrong reasons that we endanger the child's mental health.

Q. But do you really think that some of us parents here tonight are really doing bad things to our kids?

A. Not really. Most of the parents who read my books and attend my lectures tend to agree with the values and child-rearing philosophy that I espouse. You read my books and come to my lectures because you want support for doing what you feel is right even though many of your neighbors and friends do not agree with you. And I try my best to give you the data and the arguments that you need to make your case. Sometimes I catch some parents who are vacillating and succeed in swinging them to the side of healthy education. But I know that the parents whom I would most like to reach will never hear me.

Q. You seem to be against pressuring kids. But isn't pressure necessary and even good for kids? Many successful athletes had coaches who worked them hard, and many successful business people had parents who pushed them hard. I am afraid that if I don't push my child, she may just take it easy and never achieve anything in life. How do you know when to push and when not to?

A. You have posed what is perhaps the most difficult question in child-rearing. If children don't want to take music lessons, should we make them? If children don't do their homework properly, should we insist they do it over? If children are not social, should we insist on their playing with other children? And if we do decide to pressure our children, how should we go about it? Should we offer rewards, threaten punishment, appeal to children's self-interest, or play upon their guilts and fears?

These are difficult questions, and there are no simple, easy answer to them. The only guideline I can suggest is to examine your motives. Is it really the child's welfare you are primarily concerned about, or is some personal motive or ambition the dominating factor? If you really have your child's best interests as your primary concern, then pushing a child, with whatever method is most comfortable for you, will probably do no harm.

What will come through to your child is your caring enough to make the effort. Indifference is much worse.

On the other hand, if your personal motives dominate over what is in the best interests of the child, pushing is likely to do harm. No one likes to be used, and when children are pressured to achieve something under the guise of doing something for themselves but really for the purpose of satisfying parental need, they will eventually realize the truth. When that happens, children rebel against both parental motives and methods, and the result is often just the opposite of what the parents intended.

Q. What about television? How much should a young child watch, and what kinds of programs are "healthy" and which ones "miseducate" in your terms?

A. A young child five years old and younger should not watch television for more than two hours a day. That is a rule of thumb and there are exceptions, but it is a useful guideline to keep in mind. Programs like "Sesame Street," "Mr. Rogers' Neighborhood," and many of the Disney movies and programs are appropriate for young children. I don't happen to believe that the many police and detective shows are healthy for young children. The violence is even more frightening for young children than for older ones because they may not be fully aware that the violence is only portrayed and not real. Allowing young children to watch such programs puts them at risk for fear and anxiety for no purpose, inasmuch the shows have little of a positive nature to teach young children.

Q. You seem to be opposed to lessons for young children, but my four-year-old daughter takes ballet lessons and loves them, so what is wrong with that?

A. In general, I believe there is no need to enroll a preschool child in a program involving formal lessons whether it be ballet, tennis, or Japanese. I am sure that your daughter enjoys her lessons, and if she has a sensitive, knowledgeable teacher, no harm may be done. But if that is not the case, your daughter may be at risk for an injury. The bones and muscles of young children are simply not mature enough for strenuous exercise, nor for some of the stresses and strains required by ballet, skiing, tennis, gymnastics, and so on.

As far as I am concerned, all such programs miseducate young children. This is true because there is absolutely no evidence of any long-term gain to be had from such lessons and because, at the same time, they put children at risk of physical injury for no purpose. Yes, I know there are a number of cases where children have started in ballet, in ice skating, in music and have gone on to become successful professionals. But they are the exceptions, not the rule. The number of young people who were started early and who experienced failure, unhappiness, and/or physical injury is far, far greater than the number of children who started young and succeeded.

Q. I think you dismiss admission into a prestigious nursery school much too lightly. Many such nurseries are, after all, associated with prestigious private day schools, and children in the nursery school are likely to be given preference for admittance to the elementary and secondary schools. And having gone to the right private schools does give a child an advantage when applying to prestigious colleges and universities. So maybe parents who are concerned about getting their children into these schools are not so silly after all.

A. What you say is true, of course. My concern with parents' overeagerness to get their children into a prestigious nursery school is that they are doing it for the wrong reasons. If they believe prestigious schools provide high-quality education (which they do) and that is why they are enrolling the child, there would be no problem. Too often today, however, parents are enrolling their children in these programs because they believe they will start the children academics early and thus give them an edge up on the competition. Ironically, such parents, by pressuring prestigious nursery schools to go academic, are destroying the high quality of education which private schools did provide and which did give their students an edge when getting into colleges and universities.

Q. I am divorced and have a four-year-old son. My former husband and I share joint custody. Brian is with me during the week and with his father over the weekends, some holidays, and most of the summer. I subscribe to your philosophy of not hurrying children, but my husband does not. He thinks my son should be in an academic program, and he and his new wife are trying to teach him to read at home. What should I do?

A. The only thing you can do under the circumstances is to stick to your guns. You are not going to undo what his father is doing, nor are you likely to change his philosophy of education. What you must do is make very clear to Brian what he is to expect when he is with you. If he asks about reading lessons, you have to say that "there are no reading lessons in this house; if you like, I will be happy to read to you." You don't have to (and really shouldn't) put down his father or his educational priorities. All that you need to do is assert the priorities operative in your house. That is a discrimination that a child of Brian's age can make quite well.

As to schooling, some sort of compromise would seem to be in order. A Montessori school might work. It is child-centered and nonpressured on the one hand, but has a lot of academic content on the other. It is a program that might thus be acceptable to you both.

Q. I am a little worried that the kind of educational programs for young children you are advocating are old-fashioned and that what you propose is more appropriate for the 1950s than the 1980s. It is a tough world out there. Look at the extent of drug abuse, of crime of all sorts, of divorce, of competition to get into good schools, and of erosion of job opportunities—not to mention the threat of nuclear war, the proliferation of weapons, the degradation of the environment. Is the kind of education you propose really going to prepare children for this kind of world? Don't the people who want to start kids earlier have a point? After all, there is so much to learn, so isn't earlier better?

A. Your observation is, of course, correct: the world today is far different from what it was at mid-century. And the question you raise is really the critical one, namely, what is the best way to prepare children for an admittedly harsh and rapidly changing world? Your reaction, a natural one shared by many contemporary parents as well as by parents of the past, is to speed up the pace of education to keep up with racing social change.

The conviction that the best way to prepare children for a harsh, rapidly changing world is to introduce formal instruction at an early age is wrong. There is simply no evidence to support it, and considerable evidence against it. Starting children early academically has not worked in the past and is not working now. For example, in the Commonwealth of Massachusetts in the early 1800s some 30 percent of two-to-four-year-old children were sent to school to read and write. This action was prompted by parents and business people concerned about how best to prepare children for a society that was rapidly being transformed from an agricultural to an industrial economy. The natural impulse, then as now, was to start children earlier. Similar attempts at early schooling were started in England at about the same time by Robert Owen. Both here and abroad the experiment failed, and young children were not taught to read and to write.

Throughout this book I have tried to marshal contemporary evidence and arguments that speak against early instruction as the best way to prepare young children for what is admittedly a harsh and difficult world. Children who go into the world with a strong sense of trust and autonomy, of initiative and belonging, and of industry and competence will be better prepared to deal with whatever the future has to offer than will children with an abundance of academic skills but a damaged sense of self. Success in life is not the product of acquired academic skills; rather, success in life is the product of a healthy personality.

Q. I'm still not convinced. How do you know that early stimulation doesn't work? Maybe people like Glenn Doman have something after all. Many people with innovative ideas were put down by their colleagues, who were too short-sighted or narrow-minded to accept a truly innovative and important new idea. Shouldn't we give these people and their programs a chance?

A. Certainly people with innovative ideas should be given a hearing and a chance to demonstrate the effectiveness of their programs. The problem is that most of the early-instruction programs have not been adequately and systematically researched. In the long run, as in the cases of true innovative ideas, truth will out. But truth, scientific truth, has to be demonstrated; it cannot be taken on faith. To date, the preponderance of research evidence indicates that the early "stimulation" of a child growing up in an already emotionally, intellectually, and culturally rich environment with caring parents is not going to enhance the child's brightness much beyond what it would otherwise be.

I think we have to face the fact that there is money in miseducation, while this is not the case for healthy education. What weakens the case of the early-stimulation people is the fact that they are selling something and it is hard to know where the truth ends and the sales pitch begins.

Q. I know that you argue that a lot of the motivation for putting children into different programs at an early age is as much a matter of status as of genuine concern for the child. That may be good theory, but as a parent I have to face the fact that if I don't put my child in an academic preschool, he is not going to be reading when he enters kindergarten and his peers are going to be reading. Regardless of why other parents put their children in that preschool, they are going to have a leg up on my kid if I don't put him in an academic preschool. That is a real parental and not a status concern.

A. I appreciate your question, even though it is a tough one to answer. In the end, it is a question that only you can resolve. I have tried to give you as much evidence as I can regarding the pros and cons of a variety of early-childhood programs. I have also tried to detail the motivations that prompt parents to put children in high-pressure programs. But in the end it is up to you. If you really feel that you are doing your child a disservice by not putting him in a high-pressure program, then by all means do so. In the long run, your sense of guilt about not doing the right thing, and your anxiety about whether your child will make it, may have more negative effects than will putting the child in the program.

Q. My wife and I both work and we have our three-year-old daughter in a full-day program at a day-care center near our home. They are starting to teach the children to read, and Donna now even brings home workpapers on which she is copying letters. In other respects, the place is ideal for us, convenient, clean, well run, and flexible with respect to hours. But we subscribe to your philosophy and would prefer that they cut out the workpapers. What can we do?

A. Talk to the director of the day-care center and tell him or her about your concerns. Some centers engage in these practices because they feel that is what parents want. If enough parents protest, they will stop. If most of the parents don't feel as you do and you want to keep your child in the facility, praise your child for the work she is doing but do not overemphasize it. Spend your time together doing things such as reading to her, playing with her, and going for excursions to interesting places. In this way you communicate your value priorities to her and put the academic experiences in proper perspective.

Q. My son will be five in November and the school entrance cut-off date is October. I know the school will accept him if I insist and he has some testing. But, given the "age effect" you describe, is this the right thing to do? I also have a social conscience, and while I can afford to keep my son out a year, I know that other parents can't and I feel a little guilty about doing it.

A. It is a difficult decision, and in the end you will have to follow your own conscience. I should say that boys are particularly handicapped by being the youngest, and while this is not always the case, the probability that he will be a victim of the age effect is always there. In the end, I think you have to do what you think is best for your child, but you can also work toward getting the school to "liberate" the kindergarten and first grade so that no child has to suffer the age effect, miseducation at its most destructive.

Q. My child is a victim of the age effect. He also has a November birthday, but the school cut-off date was December 1, so he got in. We were both working, and it would have been a real hardship to keep him home or with a full-time sitter for another year. Now the school is suggesting that he repeat kindergarten because he is not ready for first grade. What should we do?

A. Your son is a clear victim of miseducation, and some of the damage has already been done. Given the new data on the negative effects of retention showing that socially promoted children do as well as children who are held back, you might want to insist that your son be promoted. If possible, however, I would also get him a tutor who could work to bring him along academically. The individual attention provided by the tutor can also help undo some of the possible damage to your son's sense of competence and industry done by school failure.

Q. My child is gifted and has a test IQ of more than 150. As you say, he gobbles up information. What should I do about schooling for him if, as you say, most gifted children find school boring and dull?

A. There are several things you can do. One is to ask that your child be promoted one grade. For gifted children the age effect does not operate, and they need the challenge of the higher grade. Research suggests that gifted children can adapt well to being the youngest and have no problems making friends, playing, and so on. Some schools have programs for gifted and talented children, and these programs can be helpful as well. The only problem is that the gifted children are easy to label and identify when they are singled out in this way, and that can have some negative consequences.

Anything you can do to enrich the child's experience outside the home will help as well. There are now a number of summer programs for gifted children, who really enjoy these programs and the opportunity to be with other bright children and understanding adults. If your child has a gift in a particular area, you might introduce him to a high school or college teacher in that area. Many teachers are intrigued by a youngster who is gifted in their area and are willing to serve as mentor and guide the child's readings and activities.

Q. My son has been a victim of the age effect and is not doing well in school. His young sister, however, has it all. She was born in the spring, while he was born in the fall. And she is outgoing and lively, while he is a little shy. But most of all, she is bright and is already ahead of her brother in reading. What can we do to keep our son from feeling inferior to his sister?

A. Accept your children on their own terms and try, as much as possible, not to make comparisons. Look for the things your son can do well and make sure he is praised for them. The most important thing is to make your son feel loved and accepted for what he is, rather than rejected for what he is not.

_Q_. My daughter is in first grade and she is already bringing homework with her from school. Should a first-grade child have homework?

A. In general, I don't approve of homework for kindergarten or first-grade children. Homework is most useful as a complement to class discussion and presentations. When the teacher has the time and energy to read homework carefully, it can be a meaningful learning experience for the child. But kindergarten and first-grade children still need to work on manipulatives more than on workbooks. The too-early focus on "right" and "wrong" can be a very negative experience, particularly for children who are young and struggling to keep up. There is plenty of time for homework once children have attained a healthy sense of industry and competence.

_Q_. You seem to base a great deal of your argument for not introducing young children to formal instruction on the work of Jean Piaget. How solid is his work as a basis for educational decision-making?

A. Jean Piaget stands with Freud as one of the most original and productive psychologists of this century. His studies on the development of children's thinking have been repeated all over the world, with extraordinarily comparable results. His description of the stages of development thus rests upon perhaps the most solid data base in all psychology. While Piaget did not provide curricula to be taught, his work does provide powerful tools for curriculum analysis. His theory allows us, if we choose, to create curricula well suited to the child's level of mental development.

Q. I agree with you about not pushing children, but I also have a child who seems completely unmotivated. If he ever had the structural imperative, I have yet to see any evidence of it. What do you do with a child who would be happy to watch television all day long?

A. Children do differ in the extent to which they are driven by intrinsic motivation. But all children have some of it. When children show little interest in activities other than television, they are usually using television as an escape. Their lack of motivation can stem from a fear of failure and recrimination, a fear of encountering some dangerous bits of information, or a fear of having to deal with some family issue.

An unmotivated child is a stressed child. The first thing to do is to examine the child's immediate life situation. If there has been a divorce or a separation, this can trigger the fear reaction. So, too, can a move from one home and neighborhood to another, the birth of a sibling, or the death of a beloved grandparent. An overly pressured school environment can also produce the fear reaction disguised as a lack of motivation.

You can help your child recover this motivation if you can identify the major stresses in his life and do what you can to alleviate them. In the case of divorce and death, the most important thing is to talk with your child about these events, not just once, but many times. If the school environment is too pressured, it may be necessary to take your child out of the program and enroll him in a less pressured educational environment. What does not work, and can be counterproductive, is berating or teasing the child about his lack of motivation.

Q. I am a grandmother, and a "Milk and Cookies" mother in your terminology. My children have all done well, thank you. My problem is my daughter-in-law. She is an incredible College-Degree parent. She has every educational program for young children known to man. There are flash cards, books, tapes, Speak and Spell—you name it, she has got it. My poor grandson never has any time to play, and he is only eighteen months old! Whenever he can, he goes for the Kleenex box, which is his favorite toy. But his mother is always drilling him, and my son, that nitwit, lets her get away with it. What can I do?

A. As my mother used to say, "Don't mix in." Each generation has to make its own mistakes. Nothing you can say or do is going to change what your daughter-in-law is doing. If you mix in, you will only create friction that will eventually result in your seeing your grandson less often. Use your time with your grandson to engage in the kinds of activities you used with your own children of that age. Enjoying your grandson and keeping the peace are the best things you can do for him at this point.

Q. My question is the reverse of that of the grandmother who spoke earlier. I have tried not to pressure my three-year-old daughter, Jean; I read a lot to her, we take walks together, she listens to records, and so on. I make sure she has time alone so she can learn to initiate her own activities. My problem is my mother-in-law. She had her daughter into Olympic skating when she was four and tried to get my husband into gymnastics. He fought it and always had to be in the shadow of his sister, and he has plenty of emotional scars as a result. Now she wants to get Jean started and wants to pick up the tab. What do I do?

A. Tell your mother-in-law that you very much appreciate her offer but cannot accept it. Make it short and sweet and don't go into details or give explanations, because then you will only leave yourself open to argument. What you want to do is to give her a firm and final no. Go on doing what you are doing, and if the matter comes up again, handle it in the same polite but final way. Your mother-in-law will eventually get the message that this is a dead issue.

Q. We have a home computer, and I am wondering about starting out my four-year-old son on it. What do you think?

A. It depends a lot upon the child. You can ask your son whether he would like to play on the computer, and if he does, you might show him how pressing the keys results in something showing up on the screen. If he enjoys this, you might show him how you can write words such as his name and have him dictate a story to you that you can print out and read back to him. If he shows a real interest and fascination with the machine, and it has graphics capability, you might show him how to draw with the computer as an entry-level skill, and eventually teach him computer games.

On the other hand, if your son does not show much interest in the machine, then I would not pursue it. You can always try again when the child is older and his pattern of interests has changed. There is really no point in insisting that a child get involved in computers when the child has no inclination in that direction. By insisting when the child is not ready, you may destroy any possible interest when he or she is ready.

Q. My mother-in-law committed suicide about a year ago. We did not tell our five-year-old son how she died, and he seems to have taken it well. We talk about her often, and he remembers her fondly. Now, however, my husband wants to tell him the "truth," because he is afraid our son might hear it from someone else. What do you think?

A. Young children do not really understand suicide and I see little reason for telling a six-year-old anything other than what you have already told him. There will be plenty of time for him to hear about the real manner of her death when he is an adolescent and can understand suicide and perhaps some of his grandmother's motives, particularly if she was in ill health. I must say that I find your husband's reasoning a little farfetched. Even if someone were cruel and malicious enough to tell your son, or even if he overheard it by chance, he would still have trouble comprehending it. It seems to me that your husband is still having trouble with the fact that his mother took her own life. That is understandable, but he should speak with a professional about his feelings and not impose his preoccupations upon your son.

Q. What about divorce, then—when do you tell your children about a divorce? If they can't understand it, do you just say "Daddy is away at work" and live a lie until the child is a teenager?

A. I would suggest that the two situations are quite different. The child was told about his grandmother's death and was able to mourn for her. The manner of her death is an unnecessary detail that would in no way help the mourning process. Telling a child about a divorce is as necessary as telling the child about the grandmother's death. It is important to explain in great detail what is going to happen to the child, where he or she will live, who will take care of him or her, and that though the parents no longer love each other, they still love the child.

But it is really not necessary to go into details with the child about why the divorce is happening any more than it is necessary to go into great detail about the manner of a grandparent's death. It is the fact of death or divorce we have to help children to deal with, not the causes of these events. It is our egos that are bound up with causes, not the child's.

Q. Some school systems have pre-kindergartens for children as young as three years. Does the age effect operate here as well?

A. Pre-kindergartens are, in effect, a way of providing public child care for young children; they are not really kindergartens. If the programs provided are age-appropriate, they can provide a useful child-care service for parents. On the other hand, if they attempt to "teach" children various skills, the result could well be comparable to the impact of kindergarten. The youngest children will experience failure and all the psychological consequences of that experience. I do believe that the age effect can be observed even among three-year-olds if they are in an academically pressured environment.

Q. How widespread is the kind of miseducation you talk about? Is it happening in other countries as well?

A. Canada tends to be more child-centered than we are and to have more age-appropriate programs. Canadian parents and educators, however, are experiencing some of the same pressures as we are here, and they may lose ground. Most of both Western and Eastern European countries do not start children on academics until they are six or seven, an age when most children are able to engage in symbolic and derived learning. Nonetheless, recent cross-national comparisons of academic achievement have made countries particularly aware of their standing and have stimulated the interest of the countries involved in improving their relative standing. Unfortunately, the method often suggested, and sometimes implemented, is to start children earlier on the academic track. Although this has not happened yet, the pressures are already building in the Scandinavian countries.

Japan, of course, is special because of its extreme homogeneity of culture, tradition, and race. At the early-childhood level there is more emphasis upon getting children to have the right attitude, to take instruction from adults, to work hard, and to get the job done, than there is on the child's mastering particular skills. Japanese mothers now take major responsibility for educating their young children, and this responsibility has taken its toll. Some Japanese mothers develop what has been called a "child-rearing neurosis." In some extreme cases, where the mother feels that she or the child has failed, the mother may take both her own and her child's life.

In general, we are about ten years ahead of most other

countries in the extent to which we are miseducating our young children. But because other countries often imitate the worst rather than the best of our social innovations, they are likely increasingly to miseducate their children as well.

Q. So what is going to happen? According to you, we are miseducating large numbers of young children, so what does this mean with regard to the future?

A. I have no crystal ball and am not sure that I really want one. All that I can give you is a clinical impression, my feeling about what is to come. As I suggested in the introduction, today's parents are different from those who reared the hurried children of the seventies and early eighties. Teenagers today are hurried children and show primarily stress symptoms, the symptoms of being pushed too hard too soon. My guess is that the teenagers of the nineties will be more neurotic than teenagers today. They will show more obsessions, more compulsions, more phobias, more psychosomatic symptoms than do teenagers today.

What I cannot really predict is the extent of the problem. If we wake up to the dangers of miseducation at home and at school, the damage may not be too great and only a relatively small group of children will be affected. But if we refuse to recognize what miseducation is doing to our young children, we will put a significant proportion of the next generation at risk for personality problems and for occupational mediocrity.

Q. What can we do to stop all of this miseducation?

A. One thing about our society is that when we recognize a problem, we do something about it. I think that as a society we are becoming increasingly aware of the dynamics and risks of miseducation. An increasing number of professionals are speaking out against it, and the media are beginning to reflect this changed psychology. We need to reeducate all parents to the absurdity of the "superkids" psychology and to the risks of miseducation as well as to the value of healthy education. But it is not only parents who need to be reeducated; the same is true for teachers, administrators, and legislators caught up in the "competent child" mentality.

The price of liberty, it has been said, is eternal vigilance. It is also the price of healthy education. Whenever we become inattentive to the fact that children are people in their own right, with their own needs, their own special abilities, and their own learning priorities, we are likely to engage in miseducation. Eternal vigilance to the special attributes of children is indeed a high price for parents and educators to pay, but the end result—healthy, happy, responsible, and productive young people—is well worth it.

Notes

CHAPTER 1

1. U.S. Census Bureau. Statistical Abstract of the United States, 106th edition, 1986.
2. National Association for the Education of Young Children Education Information Service. 1834 Connecticut Ave. N.W., Washington, DC 20009.
3. *Parenting Advisor*, vol. 2, 7, July–August 1986.
4. Ibid.
5. Ibid.
6. *New Age Journal*, January 1985, p. 54.
7. *Child Magazine*, October 1986, p. 96.
8. R. Lacayo, "Getting Off to a Quick Start," *Time*, Oct. 8, 1984.
9. E. B. Fiske, "Early Schooling Is Now the Rage," *New York Times*, Apr. 13, 1986, pp. 24–30.
10. Early Childhood Literacy Development Committee of the International Reading Association, "Literacy Development and Pre-First Grade," *Young Children*, 1986, pp. 10–11.
11. G. Doman, *Teach Your Baby to Read*. London: Jonathan Cape, 1961, p. 116.
12. S. Engelmann and T. Engelmann, *Give Your Child a Superior Mind*. New York: Cornerstone, 1983, p. 102.
13. S. Ledson, *Raising Brighter Children*. Toronto: McClelland and Stewart, 1983, p. 68.
14. S. Ludington-Hoe, *How to Have a Smarter Baby*. New York: Rawson Associates, 1985, p. 224.
15. S. Prudden, *Suzy Prudden's Exercise Program for Young Children*. New York: Workman, 1983, p. 3.

16. D. Rylko, *Watersafe Your Baby in One Week*. Reading, MA: Addison-Wesley, 1981, p. xvi.
17. B. Bloom, *Developing Talent in Young People*. New York: Ballantine, 1985, pp. 271–72.
18. Ibid., p. 273.
19. Ibid., p. 25.
20. J. Cox, N. Daniel, and B. D. Boston, *Educating Able Learners*. Austin, TX: University of Texas Press, 1985.
21. Ibid., p. 13.
22. Ibid., p. 20.
23. Ibid., p. 21.
24. Ibid., p. 21.
25. Ibid., pp. 22–23.
26. Ibid., p. 23.
27. Ibid., p. 23.
28. J. Eccles, S. G. Timmer, and K. O'Brien, *Time, Good and Well Being*. Ann Arbor, MI: Institute for Social Research, 1985.

CHAPTER 2

1. "Kiddies in the fast lane," *Time*, Sept. 9, 1985, p. 57.
2. J. S. Mill, *Autobiography*. London: Oxford University Press, 1924.
3. N. Wiener, *Ex-Prodigy, My Childhood and Youth*. New York: Simon & Schuster, 1954.
4. L. White, "Sports Training Injuring Children," Boston *Globe*, Feb. 11, 1985.
5. C. Rux, "Are the Stakes Too High in the Kiddie Beauty Game?", Abilene *Reporter News*, Dec. 30, 1984.
6. Ibid.
7. B. Greene, *Good Morning Mary Sunshine*. New York: Penguin, 1985, p. 22.

CHAPTER 3

1. J. Bowlby, *Infant Care and the Growth of Love*. London: Penguin, 1950, p. 16.
2. L. Lipsitt, "Babies: They're a Lot Smarter than They Look," *Psychology Today*, Dec. 1971, p. 23.
3. J. B. Watson, *Behavior: An Introduction to Comparative Psychology*. New York: Holt, 1914/1958, p. 104.
4. J. S. Bruner, *The Process of Education*. Cambridge, MA: Harvard University Press, 1962, p. 22.
5. B. Bloom, *Stability and Change in Human Behavior*. New York: Wiley, 1964, pp. 207–208.

6. Ibid., p. 214.
7. B. Bloom, *All Our Children Learning*. New York: McGraw-Hill, 1981, pp. 69–70.
8. J. McV. Hunt, *Intelligence and Experience*. New York: Ronald, 1961, pp. 362–363.
9. F. L. Goodenough, in L. Carmichael (ed.), *Manual of Child Psychology*. New York: Knopf, 1954, pp. 75–76.
10. P. Aries, *Centuries of Childhood*. New York: Knopf, 1960, p. 75.
11. L. Pollack, *Forgotten Children*. Cambridge: Cambridge University Press, 1983, pp. 267–268.
12. D. P. Gardner and Y. W. Larsen, *A Nation at Risk*. National Commission on Excellence in Education, U.S. Department of Education, 1983.

CHAPTER 4

1. T. Veblen, *The Theory of the Leisure Class*. New York: Modern Library, 1934, p. xiv.
2. C. Tuhy, "The Care and Feeding of Superbabies," *Money*, Nov. 1984, pp. 88–94.
3. E. Bowen, "Trying to Jumpstart Toddlers," *Time*, Apr. 1986, 7, p. 66.
4. R. Coles, *Privileged Ones*. Volume V of *Children of Crisis*. Boston: Little, Brown, 1977, pp. 369–370.
5. A. Toffler, *The Third Wave*. New York: William Morrow & Co., 1980.
6. J. Martin, *Miss Manners' Guide to Raising Perfect Children*. New York: Atheneum, 1984, p. 9.
7. G. Malesky, "Boost Your Baby's Brain Power," *Children*, 1985, pp. 50–52.
8. L. Langley et al., "Bringing Up Superbaby," *Newsweek*, Mar. 18, 1983.
9. D. W. Johnson et al., "Review of Research on Competition and Achievement. Effects of Cooperation, Competition and Individualized Goal Structure on Achievement: A Metanalysis," *Pyschological Bulletin*, 89, 1981, pp. 47–62.
10. R. L. Helmreich et al., "Achievement Motivation and Scientific Attainment," *Personality and Social Psychology Bulletin*, April 1978, pp. 222–226.
11. D. Sanders, "The Relationship of Attitude Variables and Explanations of Perceived and Actual Career Attainment in Male and Female Businesspersons." Unpublished doctoral dissertation, University of Texas at Austin, 1978.
12. T. J. Peters, *In Search of Excellence: Lessons from America's Best*. New York: Warner Books, 1984.
13. S. Turkle, *The Second Self*. New York: Simon & Schuster, 1984, p. 129.

14. Ibid., p. 29.
15. Ibid., p. 30.

CHAPTER 5

1. L. A. Stroufe et al., "The Role of Affect in Emerging Social Competence," in C. Izard, J. Kagan, and R. Zajonc (eds.), *Emotion, Cognition
   and Behavior.* New York: Cambridge University Press, 1984, pp. 289–
   318.
2. A. Sagi et al., "Security of Infant-Mother-and-Metapelet Attachments
   Among Kibbutz-Reared Israeli Children," in I. Bretherton and E. Waters
   (eds.), *Growing Points of Attachment Theory and Research. Monographs of the
   Society for Research in Child Development*, 50 (1–2 Serial No. 209), 1985,
   pp. 257–275.
3. B. Spock, "Kids and Superkids," *Omni*, Sept. 1985, pp. 28–29.
4. E. Erickson, *Childhood and Society.* New York: Norton, 1950, p. 79.
5. Ibid., pp. 252–253.
6. S. Freud, "Character and Anal Eroticism," *Collected Papers*, Vol. II.
   London: The Hogarth Press, 1949, pp. 45–46.
7. J. B. Watson, *Psychological Care of the Infant and Child.* New York:
   W. W. Norton, 1928.
8. C.A. Aldrich and N. M. Aldrich, *Babies Are Human Beings.* 2nd ed.,
   New York: The Macmillan Co., 1954.
9. D. G. Prugh, "Personality Development Through Childhood," in
   H. C. Stuart and D. G. Prugh (eds.), *The Healthy Child.* Cambridge,
   MA: Harvard University Press, 1960.
10. G. A. Gesell and H. Thompson, "Twins T and C from Infancy to
    Adolescence," *Genetic Psychology Monographs*, 24, 1941, pp. 3–121.
    McGraw, M., *Growth: A Study of Johnny and Jimmy.* New York:
    Appleton-Century Crofts, 1935.
11. D. Rylko, *How to Watersafe Your Baby in One Week.* Reading, MA:
    Addison-Wesley, 1981, p. 29.

CHAPTER 6

1. E. Erikson, *Childhood and Society.* New York: Norton, 1950, p. 255.
2. J. Bruner, "Learning How to Do Things with Words," in J. Bruner
   and A. Garton (eds.), *Human Growth and Development.* Oxford: Clar-
   endon Press, 1978.
3. J. Piaget, *Play, Dreams and Imitation in Childhood.* New York: Norton,
   1951.
4. E. Linden, *Apes, Men and Language.* New York: Saturday Review Press,
   1974.

5. J. Piaget, *The Child's Conception of the World*. London: Routledge & Kegan Paul, 1951.

6. J. Piaget, *The Language and Thought of the Child*. London: Routledge & Kegan Paul, 1952.

7. M. E. Bonney, "A Sociometric Study of Some Factors Relating to Mutual Friendships at the Elementary, Secondary and College Levels," *Sociometry*, 9, 1946, pp. 21–47. W. W. Hartup, "Peer Interaction and Social Organization," in P. H. Mussen (ed.), *Carmichael's Manual of Child Psychology*. New York: John Wiley & Sons, 1970.

8. J. R. Staffieri, "A Study of Social Stereotypes of Body Image in Children," *Journal of Personality and Social Psychology*, 7, 1967, pp. 101–104. N. Cavoir and P. R. Dorecki, "Physical Attractiveness, Preceived Attitude Similarity and Academic Achievement as Contributors to Interpersonal Attractiveness Among Adolescents," *Developmental Psychology*, 7, 1973, pp. 44–54.

9. E. Goffman, *Frame Analysis*. New York: Harper & Row, 1974.

10. R. H. McKey et al., *The Impact of Head Start on Families and Communities*. Final Report of the Head Start Evaluation Synthesis and Utilization Project. Washington, DC: CSR, 1985.

CHAPTER 7

1. M. Jansen, "Denmark," in J. Downing (ed.), *Comparative Reading*. New York: Macmillan, 1973.

2. P. Ruthman, "France," in J. Downing (ed.), *Comparative Reading*. New York: Macmillan, 1973.

3. T. Sakamoto and K. Makita, "Japan," in J. Downing (ed.), *Comparative Reading*. New York: Macmillan, 1973.

4. J. K. Uphoff and J. Gilmore, "Pupil Age at School Entrance—How Many Are Ready for Success," *Educational Leadership*, Sept. 1985, pp. 86–90.

5. B. M. C. McCarty, "The Effect of Kindergarten Non-Promotion of the Developmentally Immature on Self-Concept, Peer Acceptance, Academic Aptitude, Classroom Adjustment and Academic Achievement." Unpublished doctoral dissertation. University of the Pacific, Stockton, CA, 1986.

6. L. A. Shepard and M. L. Smith, "Synthesis of Research on School Readiness and Kindergarten Retention," *Educational Leadership*, 44, 1986, pp. 78–86.

7. L. J. Schweinhart, D. P. Weikart, and M. P. Lerner, "A Report on the High/Scope Preschool Curriculum Models Through Age 15," *Early Childhood Research Quarterly*, 1, 1985, pp. 15–45.

8. R. Haskins, "Public School Aggression Among Children with Varying Day-Care Experience," *Child Development*, 1985, pp. 689–703.

9. E. Lennenberg, *Biological Foundations of Language*. New York: Wiley, 1967.
10. M. E. T. Seligman, *Helplessness: On Depression, Development and Death*. San Francisco: Freeman, 1975.
11. C. Dweck, "Bases of Facilitating and Debilitating Cognitive-Affective Patterns," paper presented at the biennial meeting of the Society for Research in Child Development, Toronto, Canada, 1985.
12. T. Schwartz, "Whiz Kids," *New York* magazine, Sept. 1984, p. 42.
13. Ibid., p. 44.
14. J. W. Getzels and P. W. Jackson, *Creativity and Intelligence*. New York: Wiley, 1962.
15. R. Reagan, "To Know a Genius," *Parade* magazine, Apr. 9, 1983.
16. V. Goertzel and M. G. Goertzel, *Cradles of Eminence*. Boston: Little, Brown, 1962, p. 248.
17. Ibid., p. 241.

CHAPTER 8

1. Gesell Institute of Human Development, *A Gift of Time . . . A Developmental Point of View*. New Haven, CT: 1982.
2. G. R. Gredeler, "Transition Classes: A Viable Alternative for the At Risk Child?", *Psychology in the Schools*, 21, 1984, pp. 463–470.
3. L. A. Shephard and M. L. Smith, "Effects of Kindergarten Retention at the End of First Grade," *Psychology in the Schools*, in press.
4. L. A. Shephard and M. L. Smith, "Synthesis of Research on School Readiness and Kindergarten Retention," *Educational Leadership*, 44, 1986, pp. 78–86.
5. J. K. Uphoff, "Age at School Entrance: How Many Are Ready for Success," *Educational Leadership*, Sept. 1985, pp. 86–90.
6. P. E. Tawhinney, "We Gave Up on Early Entrance," *Michigan Education Journal*, May 1964.
7. G. R. Diamond, "The Birthdate Effect—A Maturational Effect," *Journal of Learning Disabilities*, Mar. 16, 1983, pp. 161–164.
8. J. E. Gilmore, "How Summer Children Benefit from a Delayed Start in School." Paper presented at the annual conference of the Ohio School Psychologists Association, Cincinnati, May 1984.

Selected Bibliography

Aries, P. *Centuries of Childhood*. New York: Knopf (1962).

Bloom, B. *Stability and Change in Human Characteristics*. New York: Wiley (1964).

Bloom, B. *All Our Children Learning*. New York: McGraw-Hill (1981).

Bloom, B. *Developing Talent in Young People*. New York: Ballantine (1985).

Brazelton, T. B. *Toddlers and Parents: A Declaration of Independence*. New York: Delacorte (1974).

Bruner, J. S. *The Process of Education*. Cambridge, MA: Harvard University Press (1962).

Bruner, J. S. *Actual Minds, Possible Worlds*. Cambridge, MA: Harvard University Press (1986).

Coles, R. *Privileged Ones*. Vol. V of *Children of Crisis*. Boston: Little, Brown & Co. (1977).

Cox, J., N. Daniel, and B. D. Boston. *Educating Able Learners*. Austin, TX: University of Texas Press (1985).

DeMauss, L. (ed.). *The History of Childhood*. New York: Psychohistory Press (1974).

Demos, J. "Developmental Perspectives on the History of Childhood," in T. Rabb and R. Rotberg (eds.), *The Family in History*. pp. 127–140. New York: Harper & Row (1973).

Doman, G. *Teach Your Baby to Read*. London: Jonathan Cape (1963).

Doman, G. *Teach Your Baby Math*. New York: Pocket Books (1982).

Eastman, P., and J. L. Barr. *Your Child Is Smarter than You Think*. New York: Morrow (1985).

Engelmann, S., and T. Engelmann. *Give Your Child a Superior Mind*. New York: Cornerstone (1986).

Erikson, E. H. *Childhood and Society*. New York: Norton (1950).

Selected Bibliography

Fraiburg, S. *The Magic Years*. New York: Scribners (1959).

Freud, S. *The Ego and the Id*. Standard edition, vol. 21. London, Hogarth Press (1961).

Froebel, F. *The Education of Man*. New York: D. Appleton & Co. (1893).

Getzels, J. W., and P. Jackson. *Creativity and Intelligence*. New York: Wiley (1962).

Goertzel, V., and M. G. Goertzel. *Cradles of Eminence*. Boston: Little, Brown (1962).

Goffman, E. *Frame Analysis*. New York: Harper Colophon Books (1974).

Green, J. A. *The Educational Ideas of Pestalozzi*. New York: Greenwood (1914).

Greene, B. *Good Morning Mary Sunshine*. New York: Penguin (1985).

Inhelder, B., and J. Piaget. *The Growth of Logical Thinking from Childhood Through Adolescence*. New York: Basic Books (1958).

Ledson, S. *Raising Brighter Children*. Toronto: McClelland and Stewart (1983).

Linden, E. *Apes, Men and Language*. New York: Saturday Review Press/ E. P. Dutton (1974).

Ludington-Hoe, S. *How to Have a Smarter Baby*. New York: Rawson Associates (1985).

McGraw, M. B. *Growth: A Study of Johnny and Jimmy*. New York: Appleton-Century Crofts (1935).

McKay, R. H., L. Cordelli, H. Ganson, B. Barrett, C. McConkey, and M. Plantz. *The Impact of Head Start on Children, Families, and Communities*. Final Report of the Head Start Evaluation, Synthesis and Utilization Project. Washington: CSR, Inc. (1985).

Mill, J. S. *Autobiography*. London: Oxford University Press (1924).

Montessori, M. *The Montessori Method*. New York: Schocken (1964).

Moore, R., and D. N. Moore. *School Can Wait*. Provo, UT: Brigham Young University Press (1979).

Papert, S. *Mindstorms*. New York: Basic Books (1980).

Piaget, J. *The Psychology of Intelligence*. London: Routledge & Kegan Paul (1950).

Piaget, J. *The Child's Conception of the World*. London: Routledge & Kegan Paul (1951).

Piaget, J. *The Language and Thought of the Child*. London: Routledge & Kegan Paul (1952).

Piaget, J. *The Origins of Intelligence in Children*. New York: International Universities Press (1952).

Piaget, J. *The Construction of Reality in the Child*. New York: Basic Books (1954).

Piaget, J. *Play, Dreams and Imitation in Children*. New York: Norton (1962).

Pollack, L. *Forgotten Children*. Cambridge: Cambridge University Press (1983).

Postman, N. *The Disappearance of Childhood*. New York: Delacorte (1982).

Rousseau, J. J. *Emile*. New York: E. P. Dutton (1955).

Skinner, B. F. *The Behavior of Organisms*. New York: Appleton-Century Crofts (1938).

Spock, B. *Baby and Child Care*. New York: Pocket Books (1976).

Turkle, S. *The Second Self*. New York: Simon & Schuster (1984).

Veblen, T. *The Theory of the Leisure Class*. New York: Modern Library (1934).

Watson, J. B. *Behaviorism*. New York: Norton (1925).

White, B. H. *The First Three Years of Life*. Englewood Cliffs, NJ: Prentice-Hall (1975).

Wiener, N. *Ex-Prodigy: My Childhood and Youth*. New York: Simon & Schuster (1954).

Index

Index

bonding, *see* attachment

bowel training, *see* toilet training

Bowlby, John, 53, 70

Brazelton, T. Berry, 8

brothers, *see* siblings

Bruner, Jerome, 30, 57–60

care-givers, attachment to, 98–9

carpentry area, 167

Chase, Stuart, 72–3

childhood, historical development of
concept of, 66–8

Clark, William, 21

Clarke-Stewart, Alison, 6

clockface, ability to read, 58–9

clothing, 75

cold interactions, 99–101

Coles, Robert, 76–7

College-Degree parents, 34–7, 78

commercial programs and materials, 10
for self-protection training, 42, 43

communications, attachment and trust
and, 96–8

competence, child's sense of play and,
155–8
sense of helplessness versus, 137,
147–58
structural imperative and development and, 148–55

competent child, concept of the, 30,
54–71
concept of childhood and, 66–8
current status of, 69–71
as hidden potential, 66–9
as IQ malleability, 64–6
low-income parents and, 54
middle-class children and, 69–71
in 1960s, 56–69
as readiness to learn, 59–63
as unlimited learning ability, 57–9

competition (competitiveness), 37–40
academic achievement and, 83–4
computers and, 87–9
miseducation and, 80–4

computers, 22, 84–92, 199
as leisure-class status symbols, 85–7
mental development and, 89–92
parental competition and, 87–9
programmed instruction with, 87–9

concrete operations, 148–50

conformity, sense of belonging and,
129, 134

conspicuous consumption, Veblen's
concept of, 73–6

cooperation, academic achievement
and, 84

cooperative play, 125–6

crises, psychosocial, 95–158
autonomy versus shame and doubt,
104–14
belonging versus alienation, 115,
124–35
competence versus helplessness, 137,
147–58
industry versus inferiority, 136–47
initiative versus guilt, 115–24
trust versus mistrust, 95–104

curiosity, children's questions and, 119

curriculum, competent child concept
and, 57–8

day-care centers, 5, 97

death, 47, 49, 199–200
children's questions about, 123–4

delaying school entry, age effect and,
178–80

DeMaus, Leonard, 67

Demos, John, 67

Denmark, 141

DeRoss, Jimmie Anne, 39–40

Dewey, John, 23

digital clock, telling time from, 58–9

disadvantaged (low-income) children,
63, 82–3
malleability of IQ of, 65, 66

discipline, 185–6

divorce, 200
sense of belonging and, 127–8